Anita Horn
The Human Right to Democracy

Ideen & Argumente

Edited by
Wilfried Hinsch and Thomas Schmidt

Anita Horn
The Human Right to Democracy

A Critical Evaluation

DE GRUYTER

ISBN 978-3-11-077738-3
e-ISBN (PDF) 978-3-11-062856-2
e-ISBN (EPUB) 978-3-11-062910-1
ISSN 1862-1147

Library of Congress Control Number: 2019951087

Bibliografic information published by the Deutsche Nationalbibliothek
The Deutsche Nationalbibliothek lists this publication in the Deutsche Nationalbibliografie;
detailed bibliografic data are available on the Internet at http://dnb.dnb.de.

© 2021 Walter de Gruyter GmbH, Berlin/Boston
This volume is text- and page-identical with the hardback published in 2019.
Cover design: Martin Zech, Bremen
Cover concept: +malsy, Willich
Printing and binding: CPI books GmbH, Leck

www.degruyter.com

Acknowledgements

This book grew out of a PhD thesis in Political Philosophy at the University of Zurich. The project entitled "Is there a human right to democracy" was generously founded by the Swiss National Science foundation. I thank my supervisors Prof. Dr. Francis Cheneval (Zurich) and Prof. Dr. Dr. h.c. mult. Axel Honneth (New York) for their vivid interest and support. The writing process has innumerably profited from inspiring discussions and collaborations during the months at the Columbia University NY.

I also want to thank several individuals who read the manuscript in total or in part and offered valuable suggestions, Prof. Dr. Dr. Roland Kley, Prof. Dr. Richard Amesbury, Prof. Dr. Sibyl S. Schwarzenbach, Prof. Dr. Peter Schaber, Prof. em. Dr. Georg Kohler, Prof. Dr. Ralph Weber, Alice El-Wakil, Dr. Michael Räber, Dr. Martin Beckstein, Michel Meliopoulos, Dr. Michael H. Best und Dr. Sylvia Best. For far more than editorial assistance I thank Lisa Brun.

Contents

Introduction —— 1

1	**Mapping the debate —— 8**	
1.1	Interdisciplinary scope —— 8	
1.2	The forking paths of the human right to democracy —— 9	
1.3	Rawls's long shadow —— 10	
2	**Political conceptions: top down —— 14**	
2.1	Normative political conceptions —— 16	
2.1.1	The normative idea of membership (Joshua Cohen) —— 16	
2.1.2	Yes, there is a human right to democracy—but not yet (Alyssa R. Bernstein) —— 26	
2.1.3	Realizing the human right to democracy step by step—without promoting it as such (Matthew Lister) —— 29	
2.1.4.	Human right to democracy: morally affirmed, politically rejected (David A. Reidy) —— 30	
2.2	Instrumental political conceptions —— 31	
2.2.1	Two level model of human rights but no human right to democracy (Charles Beitz) —— 31	
2.2.2	Minimal democracy as a legitimate claim: three arguments (Allan Buchanan) —— 35	
2.3	Concluding remarks: —— 38	
2.3.1	Normative political conceptions: an argument on behalf of the interests of the political collective —— 39	
2.3.2	Instrumental political conceptions: international interventions on behalf of human rights —— 41	
3	**Moral conceptions: bottom up —— 43**	
3.1	Intrinsic moral conceptions —— 45	
3.1.1	The human right to democracy is not a basic, but an applied human right (James Griffin) —— 45	
3.1.2	Empowering human development instead of enacting a human right to democracy (Martha Nussbaum) —— 48	
3.1.3	The universal value of democracy (Amartya Sen) —— 52	
3.1.4	The right to justification as a right to democratic procedures (Rainer Forst) —— 54

3.1.5		Legitimate political decision-making depends on democratic self-government (Seyla Benhabib) —— 58
3.1.6		The human right to democracy as the capstone of international law (Stephan Kirste) —— 61
3.1.7		Social democracy as a global vision (Carol C. Gould) —— 63
3.2		Instrumental moral conceptions —— 68
3.2.1		Empirical foundation of the moral claim for worldwide minimally egalitarian democracy (Thomas Christiano) —— 68
3.2.2		Individual moral autonomy needs "rule by the people" (Robert Dahl) —— 74
3.2.3		International demoi-cracy on the grounds of a legal human right to democracy (Samantha Besson) —— 78
3.2.4		The right to democracy is no fundamental human right (Richard J. Arneson) —— 81
	3.2.5.	A minimalist human rights claim to democracy: a human right to (some kind of) political participation (David Miller) —— 83
3.2.6		The human right to democracy belongs to the group of basic human rights (William Talbott) —— 87
3.3		Provisional appraisal of the moral conceptions —— 92
3.3.1		Insights from discussing intrinsic moral conceptions (those conceptions which derive human rights from assumptions of the basic moral nature of humans) —— 92
3.3.2		Lessons from instrumental moral conceptions —— 94
4		**An alternative perspective on the human right to democracy —— 97**
4.1		Post analysis: key findings summarized —— 97
4.2		An alternative view: the human right to voice —— 100
4.2.1		The moral and social philosophical justification of a human right to voice —— 100
4.2.2		Voice and exit in Albert O. Hirschman's footsteps —— 108
4.2.3		The human right to voice under an international, political philosophical viewpoint: is Rawls's consultation hierarchy a critique of the idea of a human right to voice? —— 112
4.2.4		Potentials and challenges of a human right to voice —— 115

References —— 117

Index —— 121

Introduction

The moral philosophical question whether there should be a human right to democracy (HRD) developed as an offshoot of the global justice debate in the 1990s. Within the global justice debate, authors such as Franck,[1] Ezetah,[2] and Fox and Roth[3] claimed that there was a trend in international law of growing worldwide acknowledgement of an enforceable right of peoples to democratic government. Concurrent debates in political philosophy on the limits of national self-determination in an age of globalization and international interdependency, and on the possibilities of global governance, put democratic peace at the center of global policy concerns.[4] Democratic process came to be seen as a precondition for achieving global justice by establishing the requisite rights and norms. Since the end of the Cold War, the issues of the right to democratic government have featured prominently in the discussions concerning the US, and other Western countries', policy of intervention. While, initially, the right to democratic government was understood as a right of a national collective body (the *demos*), it was increasingly employed as an argument to justify military *humanitarian* interventions on the international level of politics. The question whether there is a collective right to democratic government transformed into the question whether there is a *human right* to democracy. Reflecting the political turn in contemporary debate on human rights, which frames the philosophical questions of global justice in terms of human rights,[5] the question whether the claim to democratic government is justified from an individual rights perspective rose to the forefront of concerns. Justifying humanitarian interventions at a human rights level, rather then from the standpoint of political decision-making, gained currency in international law reasoning. The two distinct tracks of argumentation within the general human rights debate correspond with those in the particular debate on whether there is a human right to democracy. On the one side, human rights are understood to be rights human beings have in virtue of being humans, cor-

---

[1] Thomas M. Franck, "The Emerging Right to Democratic Governance," 86(1) *American Journal of International Law* (1992): 41–91.
[2] Reginald Ezetah, "The Right to Democracy: A Qualitative Inquiry," 22 *Brooklyn Journal of International Law* (1996–97): 495.
[3] Gregory Fox and Brad Roth, "Democracy and International Law," 27 *Review of International Studies* (2001): 327–52.
[4] Georg Kohler, "Otfried Höffe, Demokratie im Zeitalter der Globalisierung," in Manfred Brocker (ed.), *Geschichte des politischen Denkens* (Frankfurt a. M.: Suhrkamp, 2008), 790–806, 790.
[5] Eva Erman, "The 'Right to Have Rights'," in Mark Goodale (ed.), *Human Rights at the Crossroads* (Oxford: Oxford University Press, 2013), 72.

responding to their needs, capacities and interests. On the other side, human rights can be rather understood as practical tools of international politics ensuring minimal standards of collaboration and disagreement. Applied to the particular HRD question, on the one hand, the contrasting readings lead to an understanding of a human right to democracy in the form of an individual right to certain forms of political participation and political decision-making. On the other hand, the HRD question is interpreted as the universal collective right to self-determination and minimally democratic government. Thus it often includes political claims to establish certain democratic institutions. Within the debate, it is thus crucial to explore for each author's position whether the moral human rights dimension is distinguished from or considered as coextensive with the political dimension. The cleavage between moral, human rights argumentation and an argumentation focusing on the feasibility- and utility-arguments at the international political level additionally points to the different consequences a HRD would have on national and on international level. On national level, the HRD would require an investigation of the democratic reality not just in non-liberal but also in western liberal democratic countries. Are all individuals, also minority groups such as the asylum seekers well enough represented in their human interests? Are they guaranteed to have a fair hearing and voice in case of experiences of severe injustice? – On the international level, the HRD question throws up the question of whether democratic institutions and democratic government must become a condition for international membership and certain forms of collaboration. Additionally, the question of how to deal with non-democratic nations needs to be answered. Should there be sanctions applied if a national government systematically denies or violates democratic rights? Is it legitimate to democratize these countries? Which means and kinds of intervention in the name of democratization are justified from a human rights standpoint (developmental aid, humanitarian interventions etc.)? Emphasized in various ways, these controversial questions provide inseparable and recurring parts of the HRD debate. According to Alyssa R. Bernstein, for example, several of the military interventions in Iraq, Bosnia-Herzegovina, Somalia, Ruanda, and Albania, which were justified primarily by humanitarian concerns, were conducted with the explicit objective of protecting or establishing democratic governance.[6] Bernstein problematizes the equation of the right to democratic governance and the human right to democracy, claiming that the trend in international law to sup-

---

[6] Alyssa R. Bernstein, "A Human Right to Democracy? Legitimacy and Intervention," in Rex Martin and David Reidy (eds.), *Rawl's Law of Peoples: A Realistic Utopia?* (Oxford: Blackwell, 2007), 278.

port an enforceable human right to democratic governance extends to the argument that the international community should not recognize as legitimate any non-democratic government.[7]

Obviousely, the conjunction of moral human rights questions and political reasoning thus generates conceptual and normative difficulties. Whereas the demand for a collective right to democratic institutions entails a political functional claim for a kind of governance that protects and guarantees human rights, the human right to democracy is understood as a subjective, individual rights claim comparable to other freedom-related rights. As such, the human right to democracy must be understood as a right potentially against one's own government or people, even if it is democratically established. For example, this could be the case if a democratic government is transformed into a tyranny of the majority through the power of a people's ideology.[8] Thus, the idea of a human right to democracy acquires its normative force by being interpreted as protective of the value of individual self-determination rather than of collective self-determination. The idea includes the primary demand that human beings not only enjoy freedom, but also decide about their liberties beyond their national identity or of the place of residence.[9]

Overall, the philosophical question whether claiming a human right to democracy is morally justified is closely related, but not identical, to the question whether there should be a collective right to democratic institutions. Therefore, to have a clear view of the many levels of this debate, it is important to keep in mind the distinct human rights theories involved and the presumed distinct contents of the concept of democracy. "Democracy" can be understood either as a concrete governmental organizational structure with (at least minimal) democratic institutions, decision procedures, and the rule of law, or as a societal ideal or "ethos" referring to the intrinsic value of self-government and participation for citizens, ethnic or minority groups, and nations. Democracy as a societal normative ideal usually serves as a reserve of imagination generative of more concrete demands for democratic institutions. Carol C. Gould's global democracy ideal provides an example of this kind of approach. According to her understanding of democracy, democracy denotes a manifold social and political

---

[7] Bernstein, "A Human Right to Democracy? Legitimacy and Intervention," 278.
[8] Georg Lohmann, "Liberal and Republican Understanding of the Relationship Between Democracy and Human Rights," in Margot Brown, Anne-Marie Eekhout, and Yoanna Baleva (eds.), *DARE in ACTION, Vision and Practice for Democracy and Human Rights Education in Europe* (Berlin: The Dare Network, 2006), 11–14.
[9] Stephan Kirste, "The Human Right to Democracy as a Capstone of Law," 4 *Legal Journal "Law of Ukraine"* (2013): 144.

model for interaction between the members of a political community that serves as the precondition for an internalized and convinced habitus and shared ethos for political participation and decision-making.[10] Gould's example represents one pole of the spectrum of understandings of democracy. Other authors such as Thomas Christiano represent a distinct conception, a "minimal egalitarian democracy" including a cluster of rights such as formally equal votes, equal opportunity to run for office, or to determine the agenda of decision-making.[11] Apart from the diverging current understandings of democracy, the historical transformation of the concept has to be minded. The contemporary transformation of related political sub-concepts, such as *citizenship*, also have to be taken into consideration. For example, with regard to the establishment of the claim of the human right to democracy, contemporary democratic theory has been substantially informed by the political philosophical discussion about the changing meaning of citizenship in the age of globalization and pluralism. This discussion about citizenship addresses the importance of *inclusion* and *membership* underlying most minimal-version claims of the human right to democracy, worded as a human right to have rights or as a human right to participation.

This book provides a systematical and critical evaluation of the key philosophical contributions to the debate. It helps the reader understand the main difficulties, as well as the potential implications, of what is a most relevant contemporary debate. It synthesizes the elements of the debate in an accessible and comprehensive way, by enumerating and comparing the different premises and arguments. Without compromising the complexity of the debate, the book foregrounds the common denominators and points to unresolved conceptual problems and the overall controversial nature of the claim of a human right to democracy, which is based on the liberal democratic idea of political equality.

In order to address the question whether there should be a human right to democracy, I focus on the debate in political philosophy over roughly the past decade. Arguments that loom large in this debate stem from authors such as Joshua Cohen, Charles Beitz, Carol C. Gould, and Thomas Christiano, each representing a different thought tradition (in political and moral philosophy, political science, and law).[12] Prior questions have been raised by Jürgen Habermas,

---

[10] Carol C. Gould, *Globalizing Democracy and Human Rights* (Cambridge: Cambridge University Press, 2004).
[11] Thomas Christiano, "An Egalitarian Argument for a Human Right to Democracy," in *Human Rights: The Hard Questions*, hg. von Cindy Holder und David Reidy (Cambridge: Cambridge University Press, 2013), 301–25.
[12] The most prominent authors of the debate include: Charles R. Beitz, *The Idea of Human Rights* (New York: Oxford University Press, 2009); Allen Buchanan, *Justice, Legitimacy, and*

on the grounds of the equi-primordiality of human rights and democracy,[13] and also by John Rawls in *A Theory of Justice*[14] and *The Law of the Peoples*.[15] Joshua Cohen significantly stimulated the current HRD debate in the early twenty-first century, addressing and rejecting the claim for an HRD in his article "Is there A Human Right to Democracy?"[16]

Self-Determination: Moral Foundations for International Law (Oxford; New York: Oxford University Press, 2004), 142–147; Carol C. Gould, *Globalizing Democracy and Human Rights* (Cambridge: Cambridge University Press, 2004); Carol C. Gould, "The Human Right to Democracy and Its Global Impact," in Cindy Holder and David Reidy (eds.), *Human Rights: The Hard Questions* (Cambridge: Cambridge University Press, 2013), 285–300; Thomas Christiano, "An Instrumental Argument for a Human Right to Democracy," 39(2) *Philosophy & Public Affairs* (2011): 142–176; Thomas Christiano, "An Egalitarian Argument for a Human Right to Democracy," in Cindy Holder and David Reidy (eds.), *Human Rights: The Hard Questions* (Cambridge: Cambridge University Press, 2013), 301–325; Seyla Benhabib, "Is There a Human Right to Democracy? Beyond Interventionism and Indifference," in Christoph Broszies and Henning Hahn (eds.), *Philosophical Dimensions of Human Rights. Some Contemporary Views* (Dordrecht: Springer, 2012), 191–214; Seyla Benhabib, "Gibt es ein Menschenrecht auf Demokratie? Jenseits von Interventionspolitik und Gleichgültigkeit," in Christoph Broszies and Henning Hahn (eds.), *Globale Gerechtigkeit. Schlüsseltexte zur Debatte zwischen Partikularismus und Kosmopolitismus* (Berlin: Suhrkamp, 2010), 404–438; James Griffin, *On Human Rights* (Oxford University Press, 2008); David Miller, *National Responsibility and Global Justice* (Oxford University Press, 2007); David A. Reidy, "On the Human Right to Democracy: Searching for Sense Without Stilts," SSRN Scholarly Paper (April 17, 2012), available at http://papers.ssrn.com/abstract=2041327 (accessed August 20, 2014); Bernstein, "A Human Right to Democracy? Legitimacy and Intervention"; Samantha Besson, "The Human Right to Democracy—A Moral Defence with a Legal Nuance," Paper presented at the Definition and Development of Human Rights and Popular Sovereignty in Europe, Frankfurt a. M., May 15–16, 2009. Doc. No. CDL-UD(2010)003, available at http://www.venice.coe.int/webforms/documents/?pdf=CDL-UD%282010%29003-e (accessed August 20, 2014); Rainer Forst, "The Justification of Human Rights and the Basic Right to Justification: A Reflexive Approach," 120(4) *Ethics* (2010): 711–40; Hilary Charlesworth, "Is There a Human Right to Democracy?," in Cindy Holder and David Reidy (eds.), *Human Rights: The Hard Questions* (Cambridge: Cambridge University Press, 2013), 271–284; Georg Lohmann and Gosepath, Stefan (eds.), *Philosophie der Menschenrechte* (Frankfurt a. M.: Suhrkamp, 1998); Georg Lohmann, "Demokratie und Menschenrechte" (2011), available at http://www.georglohmann.de/ (accessed August 28, 2012); Kirste, "The Human Right to Democracy as a Capstone of Law."

13 For the detailed discussion of equi-primordiality, and the reciprocal structure of negative and positive liberties, see Jürgen Habermas, *Faktizität und Geltung. Beiträge zur Diskurstheorie des Rechts und des demokratischen Rechtsstaats* (Frankfurt a. M.: Suhrkamp, 1992), 135 ff, 162.
14 John Rawls, *A Theory of Justice* (Cambridge, MA: Belknap University Press of Harvard University Press, 1999 [1971]).
15 John Rawls, *The Law of Peoples* (4th ed., Cambridge, MA: Harvard University Press, 2002).
16 Joshua Cohen, "Is there a Human Right to Democracy," in Christine Sypnowich (ed.), *The Egalitarian Conscience: Essays in Honour of G.A. Cohen* (Oxford: Oxford University Press, 2006), 226–250.

The aim of this book is twofold. First, it intends to provide an overview of the current philosophical debate about whether there should be a human right to democracy (HRD). I show that the claims for, or against, an HRD can be classified according to a fourfold scheme: as (i) normative political conceptions, (ii) instrumental political conceptions, (iii) intrinsic moral conceptions, or (iv) instrumental moral conceptions. This fourfold thematic map allows isolating, order, and critiquing the main pro- and counterarguments in a systematic way.

Second, based on this analysis, I ask what the different conceptualizations of HDR have in common, and how their differences could either be reconciled when it comes to practical, ethical, and (power) political questions. My aim is to show that, despite the practical difficulties accompanying the claim for democracy as a human right, the normative idea of equality in having a voice and hearing independently from someone's residence status is of inestimable motivational, symbolical, and social value for any member of a political society. The claim for a comprehensive human right to democratic governmental institutions is seen as unrealistic in overrating the power of an international political regime with regard to questions of implementation while at the same time underestimating the necessary change in political self-understanding and practice of citizens and political communities forming a democratic ethos as it is needed for a functioning democratic system in the longer term. Whereas I will thus reject the claim for a human right to democratic government, the argument for a human right to democracy defined as a basic right to minimal political participation (in the sense that every individual must have the possibility to object and to claim support against the experience of severe injustice that it experiences within the political community he or she is living in), will be supported. Instead of a human right to democracy, I claim a *human right to voice*, assigning the moral competency to represent one's own interests and guaranteeing fair hearing independently of one's place of residence or political affiliation. A human right to voice would secure the individual political right to protest, individually or collectively, if a person becomes endangered or harmed within the society he or she is living in.

Altogether, the present book aims at providing an overview of the current state of research. It distinguishes two dimensions, descriptive and normative, which serve as the focal points in the debate. The normative—more controversial—dimension is further refined by raising the question whether there *should* be a Human Right to Democracy (HRD). What are the most expedient arguments to support or undermine the normative claim? Answering this question demands a systematic comparison and critique of the different theoretical positions. Using a fourfold distinction between (i) intrinsic political conceptions, (ii) instrumental political conceptions, (iii) intrinsic moral conceptions, and (iv) instrumental moral conceptions, this book maps the corresponding theoretical claims in favor of or opposed to HRD. A detailed and nuanced comparison of these claims shows that a human right to democratic political institutions has been widely rejected, whereas an (individual) human right to participation, minimally in the form of a "right to voice," appears to be consistent with all positions.

1 Mapping the debate

1.1 Interdisciplinary scope

This chapter presents the crucial controversies within the HRD-debate. It introduces the specific cleavage between practical and moral philosophical reasoning. Further, the current state of implementation of democratic rights in the Universal Declaration of Human Rights (UDHR) is discussed. Finally, providing the reference theory for most authors of the HRD-debate, John Rawls' most relevant contributions from the *A Theory of Justice*[1] and his human rights account from *The Law of Peoples*[2] are outlined.

In order to obtain an overview of the different positions, one must keep in mind that the question "Is there a Human Right to Democracy?" has a positive, a legal, and a normative dimension.[3] Comparing the different approaches that provide answers to the HRD-question requires, first, that we take into account, not only the final insights of the diverging approaches, but also the diverging premises. I argue that certain hot button issues of the interdisciplinary debate can be defused by redrawing the boundaries of moral and political conceptions.[4] For example, while many legal or political theories restrict their normative claims from the outset to the political realm and the possibility of practical implementation, others operate at a rather abstract level and tend to neglect common human rights practice. The two different emphases seem to imply an insurmountable rift between the moral and the political rationales. The task is to show that these two perspectives—one practical and political, the other abstract—are the two necessary sides of a more adequate concept of human rights, one that keeps its substance and applicability if and only if both, its ideal-theoretic normative foundation and its political implementations are combined. In other words, if human rights are understood as mere political concepts, they are bound to be empty, and if they are understood in a merely moral way, they are blind. The differences between the moral and the political readings

---

[1] John Rawls, *A Theory of Justice* (repr. ed., Cambridge, MA: Belknap Press of Harvard University Press, 1999).
[2] John Rawls, *The Law of Peoples* (repr. ed., Cambridge, MA, London: Harvard University Press, 2002).
[3] Besson, "Human Right to Democracy," 6.
[4] I discussed the historical separation between moral and political conceptions of human rights in Anita Sophia Horn, "Moral and political conceptions of human rights: rethinking the distinction," The International Journal of Human Rights 20, Nr. 6 (17. August 2016): 724–43, https://doi.org/10.1080/13642987.2016.1147433.

are visible from the start in the varying definitions of the very concepts of "human rights" and of "democracy." For this reason, I begin with common work definitions of these notions that can be compared to the definitions used by the later reviewed authors. Democracy is understood as a constitution based form of government that guarantees general personal and political rights. It further guarantees fair elections and independent courts.[5] Human rights are defined as rights antecedent to the state, which are assigned to every human individual against organized collective unities such as the state.[6] The claim for a human right to democracy must not necessarily equal the right to democratic *government*. In a minimal sense, the HRD is defined as a universal *individual right* to political participation. As will become apparent, the reviewed authors represent each different readings of the HRD claim.

1.2 The forking paths of the human right to democracy

In theory, there are a number of minimal democratic claims already embedded in the Universal Declaration of Human Rights (UDHR). Articles 21 and 25 of the UDHR[7] demonstrate the degree to which the international community acknowledges citizens' right to political participation—in contrast to non-citizens— as a cornerstone of a hypothetical HRD. The specific wordings—for example in article 21.2: "[e]veryone has the right of equal access to public service in *his* country" (emphasis added)—already raise the question of the role of citizenship and state sovereignty in the implementation of the principle of universal equality as claimed by the UDHR preamble. What is often overlooked in advocating the universal application of rights[8] entrenched in the UDHR, is the fact that these rights—even if not restricted by race, color, sex, language, religion, birth, and social status—are bound up with the condition of citizenship. The interest of national sovereignty seems to take precedence, and it precludes human rights

---

5 "Demokratiegeschichte Schweiz," Was ist Demokratie? Grundzüge und Geschichte einer anspruchsvollen Staatsform, available at http://demokratie.geschichte-schweiz.ch/definition-demokratie.html (accessed October 21, 2014)
6 "Was sind Menschenrechte? – Definitionen," Informationsplattform Humanrights.ch (last update December 11, 2012), available at http://www.humanrights.ch/de/menschenrechte-einfuehrung/was-sind-menschenrechte/ (accessed 21 Oct 2014).
7 Universal Declaration of Human Rights, UNGA Resolution 217 A(III), December 10, 1948, available at http://www.ohchr.org/en/udhr/pages/Language.aspx?LangID=eng. (accessed July 8, 2013).
8 See e.g. Charles R. Beitz, "What Human Rights Mean," 132(1) *Daedalus* (2003): 38–39.

from universally protecting individual human interests (also acts as a protection against the state authority one is subjected, whether as a citizen or a non-citizen).[9]

From a practical point of view, the following questions can be raised: How would a legal HRD impinge on how the receiving countries deal with non-citizens? What political authority would enforce the HRD, and by what means? Could the HRD be legitimately based on national, cultural, or political identity, or should it not rather be granted to every individual that is subjected to and affected by (any) political community in which she or he lives.[10] The answers to these questions seem to presuppose a general position regarding whether, and under what social and political circumstances, democratic rights and democratic institutions can be claimed as universal values that prove to be beneficial to every human being in every kind of society. Thus, the normative form of the HRD question becomes paramount. Asking whether there *should* be an HRD helps refine the more controversial, normative dimension at the heart of discussions in political philosophy. Which arguments are most expedient in supporting or rejecting the claim for a *moral* HRD? Does the
(dis-)approval of a *moral* HRD necessarily amount to rejecting a claim for a *political, legal* human right to democracy?

Obviously, the debate about whether an HRD should be claimed opens up a number controversies in political philosophy: namely, concerning the relation between (i) individual rights and popular sovereignty, (ii) majoritarian decision-making and protection of minorities, and (iii) legitimate authority and the responsibility of supranational organizations (particularly dominated by Western, liberal democratic views) towards sovereign states with different governmental systems. The formulation and practical implementation of the various answers provided by philosophers and political scientists to the HRD question requires an awareness of the underlying different human rights rationales.

1.3 Rawls's long shadow

John Rawls's contribution to political theory has become a cornerstone for the current debate around the right to democracy. In his seminal *Theory of Justice*,

---

[9] For a constructive idea to deal with the sometimes blurred responsibilities between nation state and international community, see Beitz, *The Idea of Human Rights*, ch. 17.
[10] Robert E. Goodin, "Enfranchising all Affected Interests, and its Alternatives," 35(1) *Philosophy & Public Affairs* (2007): 40–68.

Rawls conducts an ideal-theoretical thought experiment of the veil of ignorance,[11] before presenting the basic argument for moral equality and distributive justice. Rawls claims that a modern democratic constitutional state must uphold two principles of justice: the principle of *equal liberty* and the principle of *difference*, which set a standard for establishing political rights and for political conduct). A condensed version of Rawls's liberal account of a modern constitutional democracy is given in *The Law of Peoples*,[12] which extends the social contract theory into an international arena primarily on the basis of the concept of *public reason*. The aim of the text is to propose a political model, a "law of peoples," that reasonable liberal *and* non-liberal states and citizens could regard as legitimate and adopt. Public debate on political questions is meant to facilitate agreement under conditions of reasonable pluralism in contemporary societies, without presupposing a shared comprehensive doctrine of the good life on religious, philosophical, or moral grounds.[13]

The Rawlsian ideal-theoretical model—now extended into the international domain—provides a conceptualization of human rights that presupposes public agreement on minimal political (but not moral) values in the international community. According to Rawls, human rights "express a special class of urgent rights, such as freedom from slavery and serfdom, liberty (but not equal liberty) of conscience, and security of ethnic groups from mass murder and genocide."[14] Rawls explicitly distinguishes human rights from constitutional rights, on the one hand, and from rights of liberal democratic citizenship, on the other. The list of human rights he proposes is a narrow one, and it does *not* encompass the right to a democratic government or to political participation:

> The core human rights include rights to subsistence, security, personal property, and formal equality before the law, as well as freedoms from slavery, protections of ethnic groups against genocide, and some measure of liberty of conscience (but not, as we have seen, a right to democratic participation). These core human rights are the minimal conditions required for persons to be able to engage in social cooperation in any real sense, so any well-ordered society must protect them.[15]

---

[11] John Rawls, *A Theory of Justice*.
[12] Rawls, *Law of Peoples*.
[13] Rawls, *Law of Peoples*, 31.
[14] Rawls, *Law of Peoples*, 79.
[15] Leif Wenar, "John Rawls," in Edward N. Zalta (ed.), *The Stanford Encyclopedia of Philosophy* (Winter 2013), available at URL: http://plato.stanford.edu/archives/win2013/entries/rawls/ (accessed August 20, 2014).

Rawls's exclusive set of universal human rights is used in *The Law of Peoples* in order restrict justifications of war and to set the limits to a regime's internal autonomy.[16] The political function of human rights is central and binding for all regimes, since "the fulfillment of human rights is a necessary condition of the decency of a society's political institutions and of legal order"; "their fulfillment is sufficient to exclude justified and forceful intervention by other peoples, for example by diplomatic and economic sanctions, or in grave cases by military force"; and "they set a limit to the pluralism among peoples."[17]

There are many reasons why Rawls's theory continues to be a productive reference in the HRD debate; I will name only a few. First, the more parsimonious a theoretical list of human rights claims, the more likely it is to garner international consent and to be implemented. Rawls provides an elegant political theory applicable to the current conditions of pluralist societies. The second reason for Rawls's relevance is his theory's distinctive normative foundation and its liberal democratic ideals. Third, Rawls's theory presupposes two moral powers of personality—"an effective sense of justice," and "the capacity to form, to revise and to rationally pursue a particular conception of the good,"[18] which are attractive to morality-, agency-, and capability-based approaches.

Despite its apparent attractiveness, the reliance on Rawls's political theory in the human rights debate presents a fundamental difficulty: it is first of all designed for the specific audience of liberal democratic nations, and against the background of the method of wide reflective equilibrium. It takes for granted the existence of liberal democratic basic rights and liberties and the understanding of citizens as free and equal individuals. These normative assumptions concern the citizens in a liberal democratic society but are not claimed to be universal moral values. The aim of Rawls's earlier *Theory of Justice* is not to justify individual human rights but to provide an account of democratic institutions under the ideal theoretical assumption of a social contract ("the veil of ignorance").[19] Arguing from the standpoint of a rational choice, Rawls posits the

---

16 Rawls, *Law of Peoples*, 79.
17 Rawls, *Law of Peoples*, 80.
18 John Rawls, "Kantian Constructivism in Moral Theory: The Dewey Lectures 1980", 77(9) *Journal of Philosophy* (1980): 515–572, 525. Further discussed with a view on the comparison of Rawls and Hegel in Sibyl A. Schwarzenbach, "Rawls, Hegel, and Communitarianism," 19(4) *Political Theory* (1991): 551.
19 Rawls, *A Theory of Justice*, xii:
In particular, I do not believe that utilitarianism can provide a satisfactory account of the basic rights and liberties of citizens as free and equal persons, a requirement of absolutely first importance for an account of democratic institutions. I used a more general and abstract rendering of the idea of the social contract by means of the idea of the original position as a way to do that. A

precedence of "right" over "good."[20] The *moral* justification of basic (human) rights—if understood as individual rights—remains hollow for two reasons. First, within the political framework of liberal democratic people, certain values of the "good" (freedom, autonomy, equality, etc.), in which individual rights are supposed to be grounded, are already assumed to be implicit in a liberal democratic society. Second, the equation of human rights with individual rights presupposes a universally shared conception of the human "good"; however, as Rawls argues in *Political Liberalism*, even under liberal democratic political conditions of a pluralist society public consent is imaginable only regarding political values and not regarding a substantive conception of the good. Rawls's international elaboration of "justice as fairness" is based on his renouncing the claim of a universal, comprehensive conception of the (human) good. The claim of political, but not moral, autonomy becomes part of his political conception of justice.[21] Against this background, it stands to reason that the specific discussion about the nature of human rights Rawls has given in *The Law of Peoples* (1999) is a political one that includes only a minimal substantive account for individual rights under non-democratic conditions. The validity of an account of human rights rests on its ability to achieve wide international consent. By reducing universal human rights to a degree of "minimal conditions required for persons to be able to engage in social cooperation" (subsistence, security, personal property, formal equality before the law, freedoms from slavery, protections of ethnic groups against genocide, and some measure of liberty of conscience), Rawls wants to provide a most plausible account of human rights. It must satisfy the condition of having a realistic chance of garnering international public consent. This standpoint, however convincing it might be from a methodological perspective, does not account for (nor does it exclude) the more complex justification of human rights as *individual rights:* rights that every human being *should have* in virtue of simply being a human being. As soon as we aim for human rights conceptualized as universal individual rights, more substantive and human subject oriented criteria have to be brought in.

---

convincing account of basic rights and liberties, and of their priority, was the first objective of justice as fairness. A second objective was to integrate that account with an understanding of democratic equality, which led to the principle of fair equality of opportunity and the difference principle.

20 Rawls, *A Theory of Justice*, 396.
21 John Rawls, *Political Liberalism* (New York: Columbia University Press, 1996), 42.

2 Political conceptions: top down

This and the following chapter review and analyze contemporary arguments advocating or opposing a human right to democracy (HRD). I first subdivide these arguments into moral and political, before drawing a map of four major themes. An approach can be said to be *political* if it emphasizes either the logic and optimization of the existent supranational system or general political normative goals, such as the right of a political community to collective self-determination, minimal social justice, or, more broadly, peace. A political formulation of an HRD is framed and conditioned by larger international political or legal issues. Conceptions classified as *moral*, on the other hand, reason from the bottom up, as it were, and address the question of an HRD from the moral standpoint of a rational human being. These two rationales can be then mapped depending on the form of argumentation: either normative, intrinsic or instrumental. Using the resulting heuristic distinction between (i) normative political conceptions, (ii) instrumental political conceptions, (iii) intrinsic moral conceptions, and (iv) instrumental moral conceptions, four possible types of answers to the HRD question are presented. Turning to the political categories first, the political answers to the HRD question can be determined as follows:

(1) *Normative political conceptions* aim at a legitimate and just social and political order. They emphasize political ideals and principles concerning the welfare of societies such as justice, equality, popular sovereignty, or collective self-determination. *A successful normative political claim for an HRD must show that democratic rights or institutions are an intrinsically valuable precondition to realizing such principles and ideals.*

(2) *Instrumental political conceptions* emphasize the role that human rights play in international relations as political and public instruments. Partisans of this approach consider empirical reasons from a "normative" perspective and define legitimacy as practical applicability and efficiency of human rights in international political contexts. *A successful instrumental political claim for an HRD must show the value of strategic, political goals of the international community, for example, as a legitimate instrument to impose sanctions on regimes that violate other human rights.*

Political conceptions primarily define human rights as instruments structuring politics in international relations, in order to, for instance, justify war or to specify limits on a regime's international autonomy (as Rawls argues). Empirical questions and questions concerning the worldwide implementation define important criteria in deciding whether an HRD should be claimed.

On the side of the normative political conceptions, a distinguished strength in reasoning can be described in the attempt to find a reasonable equilibrium between substantive normative theory and the requirement of implementation in political reality. The debate-characterizing contribution of Joshua Cohen is discussed at lengths as it includes comprehensive coverage of the debates most controversial questions. Promoting the idea of membership and the principle of collective self-determination as normative criteria to measure the legitimacy of human rights claims, Cohen distances himself from a particular HRD claim. Nevertheless, the critical discussion of his membership idea and the demonstrated relation between collective and individual self-determination will allow a first delineation of the idea of a human right to voice. Further discussed contributions in the category of political normative conceptions stem from Alyssa R. Bernstein and David A. Reidy.

Authors representing an instrumental political focus are generally open to promoting their political arguments rhetorically, using moral philosophical arguments, but are not willing to stake their definition of human rights on a substantive moral foundation. They refrain from explicitly drawing on abstract principles of moral or political theory with regard to obeying the law of parsimony, and in favor of the likelihood of realistic consensus-occurrence in international discourse. When it comes to the conceptualization of human rights, the political and legal feasibility in terms of international relations and/or the reaching of some form of public consensus are the crucial criteria. Thus, unlike normative political conceptions, instrumental political conceptions are conceptualized independently of a comprehensive normative political theory, such as *The Theory of Justice*,[1] and they are distinctively working under a pragmatic, solution-oriented, and international relations focus. The contributions of Charles C. Beitz and Allan Buchanan are associated with this category of political instrumental conceptions. One central insight of instrumental political conceptions is that political legitimacy has to be understood in a multilateral, not only in a national context. The praxis of human rights is based on an international, global legitimacy discourse. Correspondingly, the definition and implementation of human rights depend on multilateral negotiations and specific judicial orders. The issue of legitimacy arises mainly with respect to the question how human rights can be es-

---

[1] John Rawls, *A Theory of Justice* (Cambridge, MA: Belknap University Press of Harvard University Press, 1999 [1971]).

tablished as standards of international and global authority in real terms, and how human rights standards themselves can be justified.[2]

2.1 Normative political conceptions

2.1.1 The normative idea of membership (Joshua Cohen)

While the Rawlsian account is a point of reference for many HRD authors, I will focus in this section on Joshua Cohen. Cohen follows Rawls in distinguishing between *rights founded on justice* and *human rights*, and, like Rawls, he denies that the right to democracy belongs in the realm of human rights. Consistent with the Rawlsian tradition, Cohen emphasizes the idea of (*global*) *public reason* as encompassing the conception of human rights, and claims that a human rights rationale "cannot be formulated by reference to a particular moral or secular moral outlook."[3] However, in contrast to Rawls's account of *public reason*[4] in *Political Liberalism*, in his conception of human rights Cohen abandons the idea of individuals as being free and equal in the presumed context of democratic citizenship; instead, he prioritizes the *normative idea of membership*, or *inclusion*, in a (not necessarily democratic) political society. According to Cohen, respect for the ideals of membership should become the minimal moral criterion in a legitimate political system. The idea of membership is demarcated from the right to democracy, which Cohen understands as an *individual equal right to political participation*.[5] In contrast, the rights of dissent, free expression, and conscience are subsumed in the idea of collective self-determination, and thus belong to the category of human rights—while the right to democracy does not.[6]

Cohen's emphasis on the ideal of global public reason and the deliberative, participatory ideals of membership, tolerance, and collective self-determination seems to be at odds with his rejection of a human right to democracy. However, Cohen's position might become clearer if we take a closer look at his conceptualization of "human rights" and "democracy."

---

[2] Fabienne Peter, "Das Menschenrecht auf politische Partizipation, Hinterfragt – Der Ethik," Podcast: *Philosophisches Seminar der Universität Zürich* (August 23, 2013), available at: http://www.ethik.uzh.ch/hinterfragt.html (accessed August 20, 2014).
[3] Joshua Cohen, "Is there a Human Right to Democracy," in Christine Sypnowich (ed.), *The Egalitarian Conscience: Essays in Honour of G.A. Cohen* (Oxford: Oxford University Press, 2006), 237.
[4] John Rawls, *Political Liberalism* (New York: Columbia University Press, 1996), 213, 217–218.
[5] Cohen, "Human Right," 236.
[6] Cohen, "Human Right," 238.

In Cohen's view, human rights are entitlements that serve to ensure the bases of membership in a community. Human rights represent what is owed by all political societies to individuals "in light of basic human interests and the characteristic threats and opportunities that political societies present to those interests."[7] These rights are (a) *universal*, and owed to all individuals in every political society; (b) *requirements of political morality* whose force as such does not depend on their expression in enforceable law; and (c) especially *urgent* requirements of political morality.[8] Cohen's methodological assumption is that an account of human rights must meet a condition of *fidelity*[9] to the main human rights instruments, such as the Universal Declaration of Human Rights (UDHR). Human rights are also *open-ended*, meaning that their identification and enumeration is an unending process and that there may emerge rights that had previously not been stipulated; *open-endedness* also means that, due to their abstract language, rights must always be interpreted concretely.[10]

As a corollary to Cohen's conception of *global public reason*, human rights serve as a shared basis for political argument that expresses a "common reason," upon which adherents of conflicting religious and ethical traditions might reasonably be expected to agree.[11] The claim of an equal right to participate in democracy, however, exceeds such a common standard of achievement. Despite the considerable advantages of democracy in promoting justice, the condition of "especially urgent requirements of political morality" seems not to be a given:

> Justice requires democracy: that is true for everyone, for us—so to speak—as well as them. A world with more democracy would be a more just world, because it gives people the treat-

---

7 Cohen, "Human Right," 232.
8 Cohen, "Human Right," 229–230.
9 Cohen, "Human Right," 230:
I have not yet explained how I understand "human rights" as a distinct normative category. As a preliminary, then, I will say that human rights have three features: 1. They are universal in being owed by every political society, and owed to all individuals. 2. They are requirements of political morality whose force as such does not depend on their expression in enforceable law. 3. They are especially urgent requirements of political morality. These features are suggested by the remark in the Universal Declaration of Human Rights, that human rights are "a common standard of achievement for all peoples and all nations." I also make two methodological assumptions. First, I assume that an account of human rights must meet a condition of fidelity: if there are human rights, then at least some substantial range of the rights identified by the principal human rights instruments—especially the Universal Declaration—are among them. The rights identified in those instruments represent "provisional fixed points" in our rejection on the nature and content of human rights. Second, I assume a condition of open-endedness.
10 Cohen, "Human Right,"
11 Cohen, "Human Right," 226.

ment as equals to which all are entitled. But democracy, with its equal right to participate, is not part of the common standard of achievement, defensible on the terrain of global public reason, to which global public responsibility extends.[12]

An assessment of the demanding prerequisites that a conception of equality requires is pivotal for Cohen's rejection of the HRD. Referring to Robert Dahl's "logic of equality,"[13] Cohen names three components of a right to participate suggested by the classical liberal democratic understandings of democracy: (i) equal rights of participation; (ii) a strong presumption in favor of equal votes; and (iii) equal opportunities for effective political influence.[14] Criticizing the right to participate because it demands "equal *opportunity* for effective political influence rather than equality of influence,"[15] which implies that the demand for influence is unreasonable if claimed irrespectively of one's own actions or of the convictions of others, Cohen steps back from a human-rights claim for political equality, although he has no doubts regarding the intrinsic validity, and the moral truth, of the principle of equality. But the insight that "right now, this truth is not part of global public reason"[16] explains why the human rights claim for political equality cannot become incorporated in human rights theory as a universal premise ("truth argument"[17]). Apart from distancing himself from fundamental value premises like equality and freedom of persons, the idea of *equal political capacity* is seen as standing in possible cultural conflict with Islamic or Confucian conceptions (Cohen's *bootstrapping argument*[18]). In search of a compromise, instead of the far-reaching claim of equal political participation, Cohen introduces a *normative idea of membership*. From the normative idea of membership he derives the "normative requirement of collective self-determination"[19] as the basis for any conception of human rights. As previously mentioned, the claim of collective self-determination is less demanding than the requirement of democracy,[20] but it is still connected to some minimal political claims of individual members such as rights of dissent, expression, or conscience:

---

[12] Cohen, "Human Right," 246.
[13] Robert Dahl, *On Democracy* (New Haven: Yale University Press, 2000).
[14] Cohen, "Human Right," 241.
[15] Cohen, "Human Right," 241–242.
[16] Luigi Caranti, "Human Rights and Democracy," in Thomas Cushman (ed.), *Handbook of Human Rights* (London; New York: Routledge International, 2012), 94–95.
[17] Cohen, "Human Right," 243.
[18] Cohen, "Human Right," 244.
[19] Cohen, "Human Right," 233.
[20] Cohen, "Human Right."

> The central feature of the normative notion of membership is that a person's good is to be taken into account by the political society's basic institutions: to be treated as a member is to have one's good given due to consideration, both in the processes of arriving at authoritative collective decisions and in the content of those decisions. For this reason, an idea of collective self-determination of a kind that I mentioned earlier is a natural correlate of the requirement of treating all as members.[21]

Cohen's argument concerning *collective self-determination* as a legitimate human rights claim, independent of a superior HRD-claim, is based on his assumption that the three conditions of collective self-determination can be satisfied in an *undemocratic* political context. That is, collective self-determination requires: (a) binding collective decisions resulting from, and accountable to, a political process that represents the diverse interests and opinions of those subject to (and expected to comply with) the society's laws and regulations; (b) rights of dissent from, and appeal to, collective decisions; and (c) the expectation for the government to publicly explain its decisions which must be founded on a conception of the common good.[22] According to Cohen, these conditions could also be fulfilled under a theocratic government, which permits only adherents of a particular religion to hold official representative positions or to acquire certain privileges. Further, these representatives need not be selected through democratic partisan elections, but can be elected by separate social groups.[23]

Cohen contrasts *norms of justice* with *norms of political obligations* and emphasizes the idea of tolerating reasonable differences.[24] Political obligation is shown to be partially independent (from a public reason perspective) of the moral adequacy of a government's decisions. According to Cohen, a limited degree of injustice is accepted by citizens, and it is inevitable even under democratic regimes. The standards to which all political societies must be held accountable (the appropriate common standards of achievement) are necessarily less demanding than the standards of justice.[25] In a nutshell, Cohen reflects on two possible human rights perspectives and promotes the second over the first. The first defines human rights as a form of universal truth about human beings and their moral standing; human rights must be understood as an aggregate of ethical insights resulting from the historical learning process. The second sees human rights as part of the conception of global public reason with the distinct political aim of presenting "standards that one can reasonably expect others to

---

21 Cohen, "Human Right," 233, 237–238.
22 Cohen, "Human Right," 233.
23 Cohen, "Human Right."
24 Cohen, "Human Right," 234–235.
25 Cohen, "Human Right," 235.

accept."²⁶ The difference between a normative notion of membership, which claims that a person's good "is to be taken into account" by political institutions and representatives, and the democratic claim that every human being has to be given the opportunity to participate and represent its interests within a political context is only a gradual one, since even the normative conception of membership needs to claim a certain equality of persons as well.

Cohen's prioritizing of the (moral) right to membership as a right "to have one's good given due to consideration, both in the processes of arriving at authoritative collective decisions and in the content of those decisions," and the corollary priority of his (political) conception of collective self-determination, leave open the question whether and how the right "to have one's good given due to consideration" is realized in decent societies. To guarantee the consideration of one's good a minimal right to participation, for example, in the form of a right to a "hearing" or—in Albert O. Hirschman's terminology to a "voice"—in cases of individuals' experiences of serious injustice within their community seems to be needed at minimum. Hirschman, a prominent sociologist and economist from the 1970ties onwards, discussed the logic of voice and exit regarding consumer reactions in the face of an efficiency loss of companies and of the state. His sociological reflections about the dynamics between exit and voice are helpful to understanding political participation processes in general. In his book *Exit, Voice and Loyalty*²⁷, Hirschman provides a definition of "voice" which I would like to introduce at this point. "Voice" is the act of objecting or protesting with the intention of achieving directly a recuperation of the quality that has been impaired."²⁸ The normative idea of membership as defined by Cohen therefore necessarily entails the human-rights claim for minimal participation, at least in the form of an individual's recourse in case of extreme injustice caused, or tolerated, by the community of which he or she is a member. An individual human right to voice²⁹, protected at either the national or international level, seems essential from the perspective of Cohen's conception of membership.

Although Cohen includes the rights to dissent from and appeal to collective decisions in his argument for collective self-determination, "the expectation of

---

26 Cohen, "Human Right," 243.
27 Albert O. Hirschman, Exit, Voice, and Loyalty: Responses to Decline in Firms, Organizations, and States (Cambridge Mass: Harvard Univ. Press, 1970).
28 Albert O. Hirschman, "Exit, Voice, and the Fate of the German Democratic Republic: An Essay in Conceptual History," 45(2) World Politics (January 1993): 176.
29 Hirschman, "Exit, Voice, and the Fate of the German Democratic Republic: An Essay in Conceptual History," 176.

public explanation by the government for its decisions" has to be founded "on a conception of the *society's common good*."[30] But what happens if, for example, the individual's conception of his or her own good differs from the society's conception of common good? If an adult daughter of a Muslim couple decides that her need for liberty obliges her to cast off the burka in public, or to claim free choice of her own husband, this claim seems not to be covered by Cohen's human right to membership. A necessary precondition to the right to membership, therefore, is an individual right to voice against decisions of his or her membership community, decisions that may be severely unjust or violent. Such a right is more than a mere right to free expression or non-discrimination. A human right to voice ascribes to persons the moral and political competence to stand up for one's basic interests, needs, and rights if the own community one is living in refuses to listen to, or support, individual members even though they suffered injustice or harm. In such cases, the responsibility of the international community is to support the particular individual. If such support cannot be provided in the infringing country, a way out of the unbearable situation has to be found within the community with the support of international human rights organizations. The provision of individual political security raises the question of how, and when, the international community would have to secure the conditions of fair membership and legitimate "collective" self-determination, and whether it would have to establish specific institutions, such as an ombudsman office, that could guarantee the individual's "right to voice".

The most crucial point of contention remains Cohen's conceptualization of collective self-determination and the lack of specific discussion about its relation to individual self-determination. Karin Schnebel, for example, pointed out in the spirit of Kant, Hegel, and Taylor, that normative ideas of individual and collective self-determination are necessarily interconnected.[31] The normative justification of collective self-determination depends from its function to enable the individual self-determination within the political community. According to Habermas's system of rights (which he grounds with the help of the discourse principle), the relation of mutual presupposition between private and public autonomy[32] is tantamount to the relation of mutual presupposition of individual and collective self-determination. Arguing that human rights and the principle of popular sovereignty still constitute the only ideas capable of justifying modern law, and put-

---

[30] Cohen, "Is There a Human Right to Democracy?," 233.
[31] Karin B. Schnebel, "Individuelles und kollektiv ausgeübtes Menschenrecht als Selbstbestimmungsrecht," *Archiv für Rechts- und Sozialphilosophie* (January 2008): 32.
[32] Jürgen Habermas, *Between Facts and Norms*, trans. William Rehg (Cambridge, MA: MIT Press, 1996), 84, 128.

ting the relation between human rights and popular sovereignty in a kind of analogy to the relation between the historical concepts of self-determination and self-realization, the legitimate claims for human rights, popular sovereignty (collective self-determination), individual self-determination, and self-realization are based on *democratic* opinion- and will-formation:

> So the sought-for internal connection between popular sovereignty and human rights lies in the normative content of the very *mode of exercising political autonomy*, a mode that is not secured simply through the grammatical form of general laws but only through the communicative form of discursive processes of opinion- and will-formation.[33]

Beyond the discussion of a discursive process of opinion- and will-formation in Habermas, Marc Weller further exemplifies the link between individual and collective self-determination. According to Weller,[34] individual self-determination is crucially determined by the liberal values of individual freedom and autonomy, and, nowadays, democracy. He argues that collective self-determination should be understood as a kind of "onion-concept": the inner layers represent the ideal of *individual* self-determination, enveloped (and ordered) by the outer onion skin —representing the *collective* self-determination. From the perspective of international law, the individual self-determination represents an entitlement to participate in the political, economic, or cultural system of a given state, and "might be regarded as co-extensive with the right to some form of democratic governance."[35] At a group level, self-determination is understood as the right of certain groups, such as national, religious, ethnic, or linguistic minorities, to enforce their interests. Self-determination is therefore seen as congruent with minority rights. Self-determination extended to *peoples* implies for example a unilateral right to secession, namely "to initiate a change in the status of a territory through an act of will of the population of that entire territory."[36] Finally, self-determination of *states* means, for example, the possibility to consent or disagree about international and multilateral standards and cooperation in the "concert of states."[37]

However strong the relationship between individual and collective self-determination is, its implication with regard to Cohen is clear. The question becomes: does Cohen's normative idea of membership meet the requirements of an indi-

---

33 Jürgen Habermas, *Between Facts and Norms*, 99, 103.
34 Marc Weller, *Escaping the Self-Determination Trap* (Leiden/Boston: Nijhoff, 2008).
35 Weller, *Escaping the Self-Determination Trap*, 23.
36 Weller, *Escaping the Self-Determination Trap*, 28.
37 Weller, *Escaping the Self-Determination Trap*, 23 ff.

vidual right to self-determination? If Cohen's membership rights of dissent, expression, and conscience meet the minimal requirement of an individual right to voice, they therefore also represent the minimal kernel of a democratic individual right of self-determination. Thus, Cohen's rejection of a human right to democracy becomes questionable, as the membership idea can then no more exclude the (democratic) claim for political equality. On the contrary, if the normative idea of membership does not imply a minimal individual right to voice, the individual members of a group lack basic protection against acts of injustice or violence that are justified by common interests of the membership community.

Even if the assumption of the relation of mutual presupposition between individual and collective self-determination is rejected, according to Caranti, one would still be needed to clarify who is the (collective) "self" determining the interests of a people at an international level.[38] Caranti presents further objections to Cohen's arguments of obligations and tolerance. He considers it a mistake to draw a "dubious analogy between political obligation in a liberal democracy and political obligation in a hierarchical society" and "an equally dubious prohibition of external interference within autocratic polities."[39] He further points out that the assumption that "global toleration cannot be identical with liberal toleration" undermines the existing transcultural agreement on the value of non-discrimination and equality.[40] Finally, he criticizes Cohen for being "over neutral" when the latter denies (in favor of political consensus and moral flexibility) a minimum claim for formal equality or a confession to the golden rule together with the HRD:

> More importantly, one wonders whether, in allowing the moral flexibility, Cohen is not betraying a common-sense notion of justice that is already part of a rising global public conscience. After all, the idea of a fundamental entitlement to equal respect is grounded in general moral rules considered as common to all "civilizations."[41]

---

[38] Caranti, "Human Rights and Democracy", 90–91: "
Yet, even if the preference to live under a hierarchical society is authentic, in the sense that a vast majority endorses a non-democratic form of government, there is no guarantee that elites' decisions will take into due consideration the interests of all, in particular of those minorities that would see their rights better defended by liberal institutions. If this is the case, the "self" in the self-determination would be a rather oppressive majority.
[39] Caranti, "Human Rights and Democracy," 92.
[40] Caranti, "Human Rights and Democracy," 94.
[41] Caranti, "Human Rights and Democracy," 90–91.

Caranti rightly shifts the attention back to Cohen's own aspiration, which is not to undercut growing consensus,[42] but to support it further. However, the sharp critique of "self-undermining" should itself not undermine Cohen's remarkably sophisticated effort toward intercultural mediation and conceptualization. Nevertheless, with the normative conception of membership and the rational moral assumption of "global public reason as a terrain of reflection and argument rather than a list of determinate rules, as part of the term 'reason'," some substantial premises remain open. Cohen aims for a *global* public reason,[43] conceptualized on the model of the Rawlsian idea of *public reason* that provides *public consent*. According to Rawls, public consent is supposed to work in liberal *democratic* societies. But does not *global public reason* already imply a minimal notion of democracy? If it does,[44] then arguing against the HRD by falling back on the genuinely democratic concept of public reason would certainly seem ironic. Cohen explicitly rejects the need of peoples to endorse "the democratic idea of society as an association of equals". Peoples don't need to participate in global public reasoning but only need to accept the norms of membership.[45] According to Cohen, the degree of equality required to accept equal right to membership is smaller than the degree of democratic political equality. However, the threshold between democratic equality (rejected in the membership approach) and non-democratic political equality (required by the membership approach) is left unclear. The conditions and procedures under which global public reason in Cohen's sense could be exercised require further clarification. Insisting that

---

42 For instance, the commitment to the principles of freedom, justice, and equality is also part of the preamble of the Arab Charter of Human Rights and could be seen as a common denominator to deliberate about legitimate claims of political equality. Arab Charter on Human Rights (May 22, 2004, entered into force March 15, 2008), 12 *International Human Rights Reports* (2005): 893.
43 Cohen, "Human Right," 236.
44 Joshua Cohen and Charles F. Sabel, "Global Democracy?," 37 *International Law and Politics* (2005): 797. Cohen and Sabel reflect on the possibility of a global public administration that would finally lead to the development of a cosmopolitan *demos* that is democratically organized. While they leave open the question of whether global democracy is feasible, their conceptualization of human rights allows the speculation that Cohen in fact does understand human right as a part of the idea of a global democratic equality standard:

In the first place, human-rights claims can be presented as elements of a global standard— a global public reason, itself part of the world of global politics—that sets out conditions of acceptable treatment, requiring in particular that political societies assure conditions of membership for those who live in their territory. The requirement of respecting human rights, understood as a condition of membership, does not depend on liberal ideas of person and agent, but can find resonances in a wide range of ethical-religious traditions.

45 Cohen, "Human Right," 235.

global public reason "is better understood as a terrain of reflection and argument than as a list of determinate rules: that is part of the force of the term 'reason'"[46] does not help to clarify *which* actors would have the right to take part at the level of international, global reasoning about human rights (and for what reasons). Are there procedures, other than democratic, that could structure and legitimate such considerations at a multilateral level?[47] Cohen gives only a vague overview of the realization of global public reason:

> The precise ways of exercising the responsibility of interpretation, monitoring, and enforcement—who exercises it (international courts and other institutions, regional bodies, individual states, non-governmental organizations) and with what instruments (ranging from monitoring, to naming and shaming, to sanctions, to force)—vary widely. Although the agent and reach of the reason are global, often acting on the principles of global public reason may consist principally in observing the implementation of its principles by separate political societies, or perhaps in assisting in their implementation.[48]

Measures such as those described would certainly also fit into a Habermasian conception of deliberative democracy. However, because Cohen uses a narrow definition of democracy, he succeeds to stay on the (logical) track of argumentation against a HRD. Overall, tracking Cohen's understanding of the key terms of *global public reasoning*, *membership*, and *self-determination* gives some indication of the complexity of the debate. By promoting a conception of human rights based on a normative conception of membership, Cohen's project is to enlarge the "common denominator area" under the ideal of global public reasoning *between* democratic and non-democratic peoples. From the viewpoint of this attempt at mediation, arguing for an HRD would seem biased. In fact, Cohen walks the line between giving a "light version" of an HRD under the title of "norms of membership" and aiming to recognize the boundaries of cultural, social, and political understandings by the other.

---

46 Cohen, "Human Right," 237.
47 For Cohen and Sabel's further reflections on a global administration, see Cohen and Sabel, "Global Democracy?"
48 Cohen, "Human Right," 236.

2.1.2 Yes, there is a human right to democracy—but not yet (Alyssa R. Bernstein)

Alyssa R. Bernstein's approach equates Cohen's normative political conception and his rejection of an HRD, but she puts stronger emphasis on distinct moral arguments and a direct comparison to, and reconstruction of, the Rawlsian human rights conception in *The Law of Peoples*. Bernstein adopts the classical interpretation of human rights as moral rights, as "rights all human beings have just in virtue of being humans sharing the same vital needs and interests,"[49] and she takes them to be axiomatic. The moral basis of human rights is seen as "independent of the character of any current or past international political or economic relationships"[50]. They must be based theoretically on *principles of justice*, but their legitimacy does not depend on the practical approval of the basic human rights by all states: "Regardless of whether all states have legally committed themselves to respect and secure these rights," the international community may legitimately enforce them worldwide.[51]

The strong link between basic human rights and the consequent claim for international interventions to protect them can be identified as Bernstein's most distinct (even if rather provident than logically chosen) argument against an HRD (corresponding to Rawls's).[52] She argues for the exclusion of political rights of procedural democracy from the list of internationally enforceable basic human rights, but, since they are grounded in conditions of governmental legitimacy, as outlined in Rawls's *Law of Peoples*,[53] she proposes to classify them as "derivative" human rights. To make sure "not to interpret the idea of basic human rights in a way that logically presupposes or requires democratic governmental institution (nor, conversely, in a way that logically implies that they cannot require them),"[54] Bernstein reproduces Rawls's idea of public reason in relation to his conceptualization of justice, reciprocity, reasonableness, and

---

49 Alyssa R. Bernstein, "A Human Right to Democracy? Legitimacy and Intervention," in Rex Martin and David Reidy (eds.), *Rawl's Law of Peoples: A Realistic Utopia?* (Oxford: Blackwell, 2007), 279.
50 Bernstein, "A Human Right to Democracy? Legitimacy and Intervention," 279.
51 Bernstein, "A Human Right to Democracy? Legitimacy and Intervention," 279.
52 "What I oppose is unjustifiable use of coercive force in the name of democracy, specifically, non-defensive international military action with the aim of establishing procedurally democratic political institutions, as distinct from the aim of stopping grave violations of basic human rights." Bernstein, "A Human Right to Democracy? Legitimacy and Intervention", 294.
53 Bernstein, "A Human Right to Democracy? Legitimacy and Intervention, 282, 292.
54 Bernstein, "A Human Right to Democracy? Legitimacy and Intervention, 287.

overlapping consensus.⁵⁵ The basic institutions of a just society in a Rawlsian understanding can be justified by reference to a public conception of justice acceptable for all society's participants. In spite of the variety of different comprehensive doctrines and value systems, public reason allows us to identify an "overlapping consensus" about what is politically reasonable for every society and about a "freestanding political conception" that is acceptable by all participants, irrespective of their conceptions of the good life:

> When an overlapping consensus obtains, the members of the society can use what Rawls calls "public reason" when offering justifications to one another for "laws and policies that invoke the coercive powers of government concerning fundamental political questions," and for the basic structure of their shared social and political world. Such justifications can be offered to and freely accepted by all participants.⁵⁶

Reaching agreement on a "freestanding political conception" does not presuppose procedural democracy but is framed by two requirements of public reason: the "criterion of reciprocity" and a "minimum-respect-for-justice condition." According to the criterion of reciprocity, the "terms of cooperation may be regarded as fair only if those proposing them have good reasons to regard them as acceptable to all of the participants, who are thought of as equals acting freely and not subject to domination, manipulation, or the pressures generated by an inferior social, economic, or political position."⁵⁷ Regarding the cooperation of the peoples, at a minimum, non-liberal peoples have to act reasonably and with mutual respect in relation to other states, "although they might be less than reasonable as regards their domestic structure of political and economic institutions."⁵⁸ Societies that do not accept the liberal criterion of reciprocity are not entirely just according to this conception.

In Bernstein's view, the minimum-respect-for-justice condition as a precondition to participation in public reasoning in a society of peoples requires some kind of political structure and civil society that would allow citizens to express freely and publicly their disagreement with their respective governments on matters of justice and to claim their rights. The sovereignty of a state and the legitimacy of its government depend on the fulfillment of this condition.⁵⁹ Bernstein argues for sticking to the substantive requirement of the minimal-respect-for-justice condition by *distinguishing between procedural and substantive conceptions*

---

55 Bernstein, "A Human Right to Democracy? Legitimacy and Intervention, 283.
56 Bernstein, "A Human Right to Democracy? Legitimacy and Intervention, 283.
57 Bernstein, "A Human Right to Democracy? Legitimacy and Intervention, 284.
58 Bernstein, "A Human Right to Democracy? Legitimacy and Intervention, 284.
59 Bernstein, "A Human Right to Democracy? Legitimacy and Intervention, 285–286.

of democracy and the indefensibleness of a mere procedural democracy on an egalitarian basis.⁶⁰

However, even if Bernstein denies that participating in democratic self-government has a value sufficiently great enough to justify a basic human-rights claim, she also shares the Rawlsian long-term motive standing behind the restraint: The incremental transition of non-liberal societies into liberal democracies in the process of history:

> Moreover, Rawls argues, following the Law of the Peoples is the best way to bring into stably peaceful international society of decent peoples, thus securing everyone's basic human rights. And doing so is the best morally permissible way to increase the likelihood that non-liberal societies will become liberal democracies. All societies change over time, at least gradually, and since decent societies allow a right of dissent and require that governmental officials reply to the criticism respectfully, by addressing the merits of the question, such societies may well evolve in a liberal-democratic direction, unless impeded by liberal states' ill justified coercive interventions.⁶¹

Bernstein's argument against an HRD seem to consist in part in a defense of "decency," insofar as the hope for a long-term progress, such as domestic evolution of non-liberal peoples towards liberal democracies,⁶² forbids imposing a specific deadline on democratization of non-liberal peoples. From a liberal perspective, this forbiddance is both a consequent concession of negative liberties to other states, and a sign of restraint of (militarized) "colonial," or paternalistic, interventions against decent states. Otherwise, the question of what role an HRD *could* play for citizens in burdened or outlaw states fades against the background of the relation between (non-liberal) decent and liberal states. If the "decency" of a state depends explicitly on whether it guarantees its members "democratic" features—such as a substantial political role in making political decisions, a right to be consulted, and a right to dissent—these claims could be expected to have an even greater relevance in burdened and outlaw states. The *moral* argument against an HRD in relation to the meaning that such a right has for individual human beings seems to be underdetermined.

Altogether, apart from rather insubstantial reasons against classifying the right to equal participation as a basic human right, the denial of an HRD seems to stand (at least partly) for a symbolic commitment to the principles of

---

60 Bernstein, "A Human Right to Democracy? Legitimacy and Intervention, 289.
61 Bernstein, "A Human Right to Democracy? Legitimacy and Intervention, 290–291.
62 Beitz refers to that Rawlsian idea as "an empirical hypothesis about political development." See Charles R. Beitz, "Human Rights as a Common Concern," 9(2) *American Political Science Review* (2001): 276.

non-interference and of respect for sovereignty. Refraining from a human-rights-claim, such as an HRD, that is closely related to a specific liberal-democratic idea of good government, can be seen as a strategic political move, consistent with democracy, making it possible to invite non-liberal representatives to the table where public reasoning takes place. Contrary to the rejection of an HRD understood as a human right to a democratic *government*, both the criteria of reciprocity and the minimal respect for justice equate substantive claims supporting an *individual right* to democracy if understood in a minimal sense as a claim for the guarantee of reciprocity and respect within one's political community.

2.1.3 Realizing the human right to democracy step by step—without promoting it as such (Matthew Lister)

In his article, "There is no human right to democracy. But may we promote it anyway?,"[63] Matthew Lister addresses a widespread readers' disappointment with the Rawlsian rejection of the human right to democracy. Rawls rejects the HRD despite simultaneously upholding the claim that democracy is required for justice and that it provides many important advantages for the protection of human rights and participation in the international community.[64] Although he affirms the view that what the international community can demand is that a state respect human rights, but not that it establish a system of democratic government, Lister mediates between the positions in favor of and against the claim of a human right to democratic institutions. He suggests that there are legitimate interventions aiming at promoting democratic structures in non-democratic states without having to claim an HRD. In classifying states according to their level of democratic development, Lister uses three sets of examples to illustrate the ways of promoting democracy without running the danger of illegitimate interventionism. First, he proposes that certain general-purpose international bodies with membership open to all states (such as the United Nations, the World Trade Organization, or the International Labor Organization) could limit or condition membership, and the benefits it entails, on the requirement of certain basic liberal democratic principles. Hereby, he supports placing higher standards (compared to the Rawlsian minimal standard for decent societies) on would-be members of organization such as the European Union. Lister advocates

---

[63] Matthew J. Lister, "There Is No Human Right to Democracy," 48(2) Stanford Journal of International Law (2012): 257–276.
[64] Lister, "There Is No Human Right to Democracy," 276.

such higher standards as – to the extent that membership in such groups is seen as beneficial – he expects them to induce democratization without being an intervention.[65] Further, a particular condition could be placed on the signing of bilateral or multilateral investment or defense treaties.[66] As another way of promoting democracy in a way compatible with the Rawlsian view, Lister names "encouragement of cultural exchange and educational visits by different members of society in the society targeted for reform"[67]. For example, such programs can involve reciprocal facilitation of travel between states for pleasure or business reasons. Exchange programs for government officials, teachers, students, and others are also seen as "useful means of promoting democracy". [68] Whereas the attractiveness of democratic life needs direct visits in liberal countries, or, as Lister suggests the stationing of Peace Corps volunteers in non-democratic countries, the promotion of democracy in the political arena needs much more prudence. Lister proposes careful but reliable support of states or political parties at the time of elections. Offering neutral provision of technical assistance for elections, or independent election monitoring, could help realizing this third direction of impact in promoting democratic development.[69]

2.1.4. Human right to democracy: morally affirmed, politically rejected (David A. Reidy)

David A. Reidy continues the Rawlsian tradition by making explicit the unresolved tension between the basic moral desirability of the HRD and its rejection for political reasons—as in Cohen's and Bernstein's arguments. Reidy starts out by drawing a clear distinction between a *universal moral right to democracy*, which he supports, and a legal *human right to democratic political institutions possessed by each and all persons against the state to which they belong*, which he rejects. Reidy suggests that an explicit assertion of a universal, justice-based moral right to democratic institutions does not necessarily imply its transformation into a *human right* to democracy.[70] Human rights must represent a "universal moral right, fidelity to which is a necessary condition of a polity's recognition, status, membership, or full participation within the international com-

---

65 Lister, "There Is No Human Right to Democracy," 271.
66 Lister, "There Is No Human Right to Democracy," 271.
67 Lister, "There Is No Human Right to Democracy," 271.
68 Lister, "There Is No Human Right to Democracy," 271–272.
69 Lister, "There Is No Human Right to Democracy," 272.
70 Reidy, "On the Human Right to Democracy," 181.

munity, or at least its central institutions and law-making practices."[71] One way to preserve their special status in international community is to limit coercion and maximize peace in international relations with publicly shared principled deontic criteria.[72]

According to Reidy, suggesting that, as a matter of legal rights within international law, there is a human right to some meaningful measure of political participation does also not necessarily amount to an HRD to democratic political institutions.[73] To amount to a human right, the moral substance of a human right to democratic political institutions would have to be conclusively identified as being of special significance or of concern for the international community.[74] Reidy denies that possibility by criticizing both William Talbott, who argues that legitimate political authority must aim at the common good of the subjected individuals, and Thomas Christiano, who makes an empirical point of showing the positive effect of democratic political institutions and the fulfillment of basic human rights, for adopting a selective, incomplete perspective with regard to the international function of human rights.[75] Both of these accounts will be discussed in more detail in the sections about moral intrinsic and moral instrumental conceptions in part 3.

2.2 Instrumental political conceptions

2.2.1 Two level model of human rights but no human right to democracy (Charles Beitz)

Charles Beitz advocates the idea that human rights should be defined as a political construction stemming from the aftermath of World War II. In his article *Human Rights as a Common Concern*[76], he detaches the classical philosophical interpretation interlinking human rights and moral rights in natural law tradition. Beitz does not consider the linkage between human rights and moral rights to be a necessary component of justifying universal human rights. A relation between human rights and moral rights and beliefs is possible, "but it would be an

---

71 Reidy, "On the Human Right to Democracy," 177.
72 Reidy, "On the Human Right to Democracy," 201.
73 Reidy, "On the Human Right to Democracy," 178.
74 Reidy, "On the Human Right to Democracy," 198.
75 Reidy, "On the Human Right to Democracy," 198.
76 Charles R. Beitz, "Human Rights As A Common Concern," The American Political Science Review 9, Nr. 2 (2001): 269–82.

error to identify these more fundamental moral beliefs with a political doctrine of human rights."[77] Beitz uses "Asian values", "the Islamic oppression of women", and female genital mutilation, he underpins that local moralities sometimes turn out to be irreconcilable with international human rights.[78] He substantiates the insight that the UDHR and the International Covenant on Civil and Political Rights are not and do not have to be seen as entirely culturally or politically neutral and impartial. The UDHR is a negotiated agreement fulfilling several important roles in international relations, such as (a) constraining the domestic constitutions of states and the fundamental rules of international organizations and regimes; (b) prescribing goals for social development applicable to all contemporary societies; (c) offering the grounds of appeal in situations of human rights infringement by a range of international and transnational actors—not just governments but also officials of international institutions and nongovernmental organizations acting in their capacity as citizens of global society.[79]

Beitz does not propagate the Rawlsian "hypothesis about political development" because, in his view, it reduces human rights to a function of legitimizing military interventions. In contrast to the Rawlsian approach, Beitz insists that to be justified, human rights should be acceptable to reasonable individuals, not groups.[80] The way Beitz refrains from a human right to democracy therefore differs, for example, from Bernstein's interpretation, insofar as Beitz argues on behalf of persons (even though, like Bernstein's, his approach is pragmatic). For example, in the case of a fictional authoritarian regime in which a minority claims democratic reform by invoking the Covenant on Civil and Political rights (whereas the majority repudiates democratic reform), Beitz argues, an international intervention would rely on unjustified paternalism.[81] The three possible arguments to justify a paternalistic intervention[82] that involves coercive interfer-

---

77 Beitz, "Common Concern," 277.
78 Beitz, "Common Concern," 271.
79 Beitz, "Common Concern," 277.
80 Beitz, "Common Concern," 277.
81 Beitz, "Common Concern," 278.
82 Normally, the justification of a paternalistic choice has at least three elements: (1) a claim that the subject is unable to choose rationally for himself owing to a failure of reason or will; (2) evidence that the choice is guided by knowledge of the subject's own interests, to the extent they can be known, or by a reasonable conception of the interests it would be rational for the subject to have; and (3) a reasonable expectation that the subject will come to agree that the agent's choices on his behalf are the best that could be made under the circumstances. In my example, because a significant portion or even a majority of the population does not share democratic political values, for this portion of the population the second element (and possibly the

ence in some people's liberty cannot be seen as a given. The "urgency of the interests at stake" of the rebellious minority has to be examined in relation to the "costs of interference and its probability of success." As Beitz states:

> [I]f a significant portion of the population lacks democratic sympathies, then it is not likely that democratic institutions will be sustained even if a democratic insurgency attains its immediate objectives. In that case it could be true both that there is a human right to democratic institutions and that interference in support of a prodemocratic insurgency would be wrong.[83]

Given the complex historical and social process leading up to institutional change and a shift in political belief, Beitz refrains from a *categorical* conclusion about the sufficiency of democratic reform.[84] He returned to this earlier position and elaborated it in his book *Idea of Human Rights:*[85] taking inspiration from Joshua Cohen, he concluded with a discussion of a human right to collective self-determination (replacing the HRD claim). The "double" normative requirement of an HRD to protect the underlying interests of the politically subjected, and prescribe a particular kind of institutional purpose, has to be questioned empirically. Given the second normative requirement, two common instrumental justifications cannot be empirically verified. On the one hand, the advantage of policy performance in democratic regimes is inconclusive from an empirical perspective and dependent on contingent social and economic factors. On the other hand, the success of democratic transitions is challenging and hardly predictable. More specifically, there is a greater instability of transitional regimes in poor societies. [86] Similar to Cohen and Bernstein, Beitz does not call the familiar justification of democracy in standard cases into question; instead, he challenges the idea that this justification extends to all contemporary societies.[87] He further seems to coincide with Cohen in categorizing a right of collective self-determination to be "a better candidate for a human right to regulate the political constitutions of societies."[88] Gathering Cohen's three features of self-determination,[89]

---

third) of the justification would fail. The interference does not appear to take seriously the moral beliefs of those whom it coerces. Beitz, "Common Concern," 278.
83 Beitz, "Common Concern," 279.
84 Beitz, "Common Concern," 279.
85 Charles R. Beitz, *Idea of Human Rights*, (New York: Oxford University Press, 2009) 174–186.
86 Beitz, *Idea of Human Rights*, 177–180.
87 Since human rights must be both universal and action-guiding, the proper inference from the fact that there are circumstances in which the absence of democratic institutions would not generate (even pro tanto) reasons for outside agents to act is that the doctrine of human rights should not embrace such a right. Beitz, *Idea of Human Rights*, 185.
88 Beitz, *Idea of Human Rights*, 185.

and understanding the right of collective self-determination to be, among other things, "a right not to be (forced to be) democratic,"[90] he concludes with three developments of the discussed claim for a human right of collective self-determination. First, he claims that the requirement that societies be self-determining is too demanding to be precisely formulated for practical human-rights purposes, and it goes against the classical international law doctrine that political constitutions are subordinate to a given country's domestic jurisdiction. Second, the human right to collective self-determination would have to face similar empirical uncertainties as those faced by the HRD. Third, claiming a human right to collective self-determination is equivalent to fostering democratic institutions as an important goal of international political action:

> To agree that there is a human right of collective self-determination is to agree that violations provide reasons for political action. In social circumstances in which the satisfaction of this right can only come about through democratic institutions, threats to such institutions would supply reasons for outside agents to defend them.[91]

In the end, Beitz fails to clarify his position regarding a human right to collective self-determination. On the one hand, he seems to propose an attractive compromise, but, on the other, he never resolves the basic issues of justification of such a right. The human right to collective self-determination presupposes already strong democratic premises.

Overall, Beitz's analysis constitutes a nuanced, pragmatic approach that is able to address contemporary challenges and empirical issues concerning the phenomenon of democracy and human rights. However, there seems to be a gap between his explicit renouncement of distinct moral philosophical conceptions of justifying human rights in favor of a politically constructed human rights conception, the justification of which depends on practical benefits and various functions in terms of international relations, on the one hand, and his implication of a kind of "side track" justification of human rights from the perspective of persons. Despite his adoption of a practical international approach he borrows from a (not further explained) moral perspective, allowing him to introduce a moral principle of cultural deference[92] or a conception of moral paternalism in a self-evident way. Such a twofold justification tries to absorb part of the fundamental tension of the contemporary political situation: The opportunity to partic-

---

89 Cohen, "Human Right," 228.
90 Beitz, *Idea of Human Rights*, 182.
91 Beitz, *Idea of Human Rights*, 186.
92 Beitz, "Common Concern," 274.

ipate in public affairs, on the one hand, should be granted to all citizens; on the other hand, there seems to be a trend of international law to recognize a universal right to democratic institutions in a top-down way. However, in his comprehensive human-rights theory in *The Idea of Human Rights*, Beitz establishes a distinction between two levels of understanding and implementing human rights. At first instance, human rights are understood as claims against the state (first level). Provided that the state neglects its obligation to protect the citizens' interests, this protection falls under the responsibility of the international community (second level).[93] Such splitting of responsibilities is valuable pragmatically—even if it does not resolve the tension between moral and political justifications of human rights. The model unwittingly expresses the fundamental interdependency between moral and political rationales already in the beginning when Beitz elaborates a distinct political, instrumental conception of human rights. The hereby expressed interdependency of moral and political rationales and its meaning for the specific HRD will further occupy us when talking about the intrinsic moral conceptions of authors who are particularly oriented to models of deliberative democracy.

2.2.2 Minimal democracy as a legitimate claim: three arguments (Allan Buchanan)

Allan Buchanan is a political philosopher and philosopher of international law who is dealing with human rights concerns not just from the theoretical but also from the practical side. Active as a member of the Tucson Samaritans, he is engaged in the support of Mexican migrants on the borders of Sonoran Desert. This active moral prioritizing of practical humanitarian support over the previous legal incorporation of human rights is mirrored also in his theoretical account in which the moral and the legal dimension of human rights can exist independently from each other.[94]

According to Buchanan, the question whether a right to democratic participation, and hence a right to participate in democratic institutions, is a human right, requires moral theories to answer two central questions about democracy: (1) Should international law include the requirement that individual states be governed democratically (and, if so, should this requirement take the form

---

93 Beitz, *Idea of Human Rights*, 106–117.
94 Allen Buchanan, *Justice, Legitimacy, and Self-Determination: Moral Foundations for International Law* (Oxford: Oxford University Press, 2004), 145.

of an international legal human right to democratic governance ascribed to individuals, and what understanding of democracy should it employ)?
(2) Is democracy (in some form) a requirement for the legitimacy of the international legal system itself, that is, must the system be democratic for it to be morally justifiable and for the legitimate enforcement of its rules)?[95]

Focusing on the first question, Buchanan discusses three main arguments in favor of international law requiring the governments of states to be democratic:

> The first provides support for the conclusion that democratic governance is a human right properly speaking by grounding democracy in equal consideration for persons. The second, instrumental argument, contends that democracy ought to be required of governments because democratic governance is the most reliable way of ensuring that human rights properly speaking are respected. The third holds that only if governments are democratic is it appropriate to treat them as agents of their peoples and hence as legitimate.[96]

In addition to the moral argument in favor of the HRD (1), he provides an empirical (2), and further a logical argument (3). Underlying the first claim (the equal consideration of persons argument) is the *moral equality principle*, which, Buchanan suggests, is the best justification for human rights in general. Despite his international focus, Buchanan thereby holds on to an inseparability of moral and politically normative claims. Democracy is seen as an important element of the institutional recognition of the equality of persons, fostering equal consideration of interests such as respect for autonomy and concern for wellbeing by requiring that all persons have the same fundamental status and are considered as equal participants in political decision-making in their societies.[97]

The second argument (the instrumental argument) asserts the instrumental value of democracy in the protection of human rights which "ought to be required of all governments as a condition of their legitimacy under international law."[98] Citing Amartya Sen's finding that democratic governments' expectable

---

[95] Buchanan, *Justice, Legitimacy, and Self-Determination: Moral Foundations for International Law*, 142.
[96] Buchanan, *Justice, Legitimacy, and Self-Determination: Moral Foundations for International Law*, 142.
[97] Buchanan, *Justice, Legitimacy, and Self-Determination: Moral Foundations for International Law*, 143.
[98] Buchanan, *Justice, Legitimacy, and Self-Determination: Moral Foundations for International Law*, 143. Henry Shue formulated that argument in a widely known version. For Shue, basic rights are only those the enjoyment of which is essential to the enjoyment of all other rights, irrespectively of whether their enjoyment is also valuable in itself. Political participation, like freedom of physical movement or liberty of economic participation, is a basic right, because

accountability prevents them from persisting in the mismanagement that is a key contributing factor in famines, Buchanan underlines the role of democracy in safeguarding the right to subsistence resources and thus to the general protection of human rights.[99] Buchanan further refers to the democratic peace hypothesis, which states that democracies tend not to make war with each other and therefore reduce the violation of human rights.

The third argument (the agency argument) carries the normative claim that governments have to represent, and serve as the agents of, their citizens. International law should require states to be democratic because democratic institutions are necessary positioned within the international political system so as to reach state consent and enhance the moral value of consensual decisions.[100]

Whereas the first argument shows that the HRD is a *moral* human right, the second and the third support its inclusion to the list of international *legal* human rights. By making this clear distinction, Buchanan can postulate that, in general, it is possible for both moral and legal human rights to exist independently of each other's counterpart:

> In some cases, the best justification for recognizing a legal right to X is not that it is the legal counterpart of a moral right to X, but rather that including X as a legal right best serves to protect some moral right Y or, in the case of the third argument, to ensure that appropriate conditions of agency or representation are satisfied.[101]

By losing the necessary linkage between moral and legal human rights, Buchanan enhances the practical possibilities of justifying human rights. One does not have to decide on a ultimative way in order to claim for a right to be a human right or to choose between either instrumental or intrinsic justifications. Thus, Buchanan says that the case for an HRD is reasonably strong because positive arguments for democracy can be advanced from three directions: equal-consideration-of-persons argument, the instrumental argument, and the agency argument. The minimal conception of democracy he then suggests includes as a key notion the accountability of the government towards its citizens. Buchanan's conception of democracy is constitutional, "with entrenched civil and political rights that provide constraints on majoritarian decision-making."[102] The condi-

---

its enjoyment is seen as an integral part of enjoyment of rights in general. Henry Shue, *Basic Rights. Subsistence, Affluence, and U.S. Foreign Policy* (Princeton: Princeton University Press, 1980), 67, 82.
99 Buchanan, *Justice*, 143–144.
100 Buchanan, *Justice*, 144.
101 Buchanan, *Justice*, 145.
102 Buchanan, *Justice*, 146.

tions of accountability are threefold: (i) there must be representative, majoritarian institutions for making the most general and important laws, such that no competent individual is excluded from participation, (ii) the highest government officials must be elected to representative bodies, accountable to the people, and subject to removal from office, and (iii) there needs to be a modicum of institutionally secured freedom of speech, association, and assembly required for reasonably free deliberation about political decisions and for the formation and functioning of political parties.[103] The minimal conception of democracy includes these three elements as requirements for the recognition of legitimacy of any state, and it represents the content of the HRD claim. Buchanan further proposes that new entities seeking recognition as sovereign states, including those formed by secession, should be required to satisfy this minimal democracy criterion.[104]

Buchanan's pragmatic account accommodates several ways of strengthening the role and legitimacy of human rights as an efficient tool for structuring and norm international as well as domestic politics. Although highly prized, the moral foundation of human rights is kind of a "normatively nourishing accomplishment" strengthening human-rights-claims; it is a necessary, albeit not sufficient, condition to justify what falls under the term. I want to point out that the flexibility and public-reason-accessibility of Buchanan's conception of human rights is convincing especially by taking it as a given that human rights, in general, and the HRD in particular, have to be seen as complexes characterized by the genuine moral, political, and legal content.

2.3 Concluding remarks:

The authors discussed above define and interpret the concepts of democracy and human rights in different ways. The comparison between political normative and political instrumental accounts shed light on a variety of possible conceptual relations between democracy and human rights. The question of whether there should be a HRD is answered differently depending on whether moral, political or legal arguments get prioritized. At this point, the results can be recapitulated for the two types of political conception: normative and instrumental.

---

103 Buchanan, *Justice*, 146.
104 Buchanan, *Justice*, 147.

2.3.1 Normative political conceptions: an argument on behalf of the interests of the political collective

All the authors discussed in this chapter reject the HRD. Cohen doubts that the consensus on the HRD's underlying principle of political equality can be reached by a global public reason. He substitutes the HRD with his normative idea of membership and a claim for collective self-determination. We owe the distinction between human rights and rights of justice mainly to political normative conceptions like Rawls's and Cohen's, who insist on only a minimal range of human rights for reasons of political feasibility and differences in political culture. Following a specific understanding of collective self-determination ("the onion-concept"), I criticized that notion of collective self-determination which is itself dependent on minimal political equality and cannot be claimed in a consistent way without also claiming a human right to individual self-determination—in the sense of our right to individual voice—within the social and political community in which a person lives (what corresponds to a minimal HRD claim). The normative value of the right to collective self-determination (a principle that often leads to the *rejection* of the claim for a human right to democratic institutions) has been shown as being closely intertwined with the concept of minimal individual self-determination. If the normative value of *collective* self-determination is to be understood as being legitimized by the normative value of *individual* self-determination, the question arises what basic human right corresponds to the claim for individual self-determination. I suggest that a minimal democratic right to participation in the form of individual recourse via the right to voice can function as a vehicle representing the human rights relevance of individual self-determination. My point is that every individual must possess a minimal degree of self-determination—in the form of recourse and probably a correlating right to exit from one's society. This minimal self-determination is necessary for the individual's free interpretation and realization of his/her own basic needs and interests within any community. In this sense, a minimal right to self-determination must be a the heart of collective self-determination, for only so can there be certainty the individual's interests are truly taken into account. Only on the basis of an individual human right to self-determination, in at least this minimal sense, can a human-rights-claim for collective self-determination be made in a consistent way.

In my criticism of Cohen, it remained open on what principle other than the principle of minimal democratic equality, Cohen's normative idea of membership could effectively be based. In another way, more explicit than Cohen's, Bernstein claims that—given the strong link between human rights and the claim of international interventions to protect them—a legal HRD in contemporary global political context would entail such a strong violation of the principle of non-interference and sovereignty that it would endanger the idea of a democratic world-peace. Bernstein justifies her distancing from the legal HRD claim by invoking the belief in an incremental historical development towards democratization; at the same time she does not question the normative belief and the relevance of democratic rights for a humane life. Likewise, resolving the paradox between the Rawlsian reservations toward the HRD and the claim that democratic structures are required to realize justice in a society, Lister proposes several low-threshold measures to promote democracy in non-democratic countries without the need to demand a human right to democratic institutions. Such a middle way is helpful in terms of practical realization of democratic development. However, apart from the pragmatically useful solution, the paradox in argumentation is not fully accounted for.

In contrast to these approaches, Reidy's normative political (but not moral) conceptions are more distinctly formulated: whereas the *moral* human right to democracy *should* be approved (at least in terms of a minimal meaningful political participation), the legal human right to democratic *institutions* cannot be reasonably demanded in our world. The priority of the political and the legal function of human rights in argumentation, but also the failure to prove that a human right to democratic institutions would actually help rather than hinder universal political aims (such as collective self-determination, world peace, freedom, and justice) plays a decisive role in Reidy's conclusive rejection of the HRD claim.

In addition to reflecting on political and legal limits of implementation of a HRD claim, however, I suggest that the moral claim for a minimal (individual) *human rights demand to voice* within one's own community is already implicit in Cohen's account of the right to membership and in the individual's right of dissent from collective decisions, and also in terms of Bernstein's norms of minimal-respect and the condition of reciprocity. Lister's approach provides practical measures for promoting democracy that can be interpreted as (non-military) interventions aimed at fostering self-determination and by extension the right to voice of individuals and minorities. The right to voice is also compatible with Reidy's account due to his affirmation of a human right to some meaningful measure of political participation.

2.3.2 Instrumental political conceptions: international interventions on behalf of human rights

Beitz separated the question of whether there is a human right to democratic individual rights from the question whether there is a human right to be governed democratically that is to say: a right to democratic institutions. For instance, he strengthens the representation of the interests of the individual member if opposed to those of the social community, and he explicitly links the human right to collective self-determination to the international obligation to protect interests of those politically oppressed. Human rights violations must result in political action but only after weighing up the individuals and the common social interests. Beitz is focused on elaborating actual measures and the institutional implementation of human rights. He introduces an elaborate two-level model aiming to distribute the responsibility for human rights implementation between the national and international levels. Apart from distinguishing between the two levels of human rights and correlating responsible actors implementing them, Beitz defines the UDHR as a negotiated agreement and identifies its two instrumental functions. First, human rights are understood to be individual claims against the state the task of which is to protect them; second, in the event that states neglect their duty to protect human rights, the international community becomes responsible for protecting the citizens' human rights. The second-level enactment by the international community is crucial for the political role of the UDHR. It allows the international political community, for example, to constrain domestic institutions of states.

Buchanan also highlighted the instrumental value of an HRD in international law. He claims that the inclusion in legal international law of a human right to a minimally democratic government is a necessary prerequisite for accountability of any government towards its citizens. Civil and political rights are critical because they provide constraints on majoritarian decision-making. Further, Buchanan's view included a minimal-democracy criterion, which sees collective self-determination as necessarily based on an—at least minimal—individual self-determination. As democracy in some form, therefore, is a requirement for the legitimacy of the international legal system itself (if that system wants to be morally justifiable in enforcing its rules), such minimal democratic accountability must be required of every would-be member state. However, whatever the political instrumental argumentations conclude in this section: they all argue from the priority of the political, legal function of human rights in the framework of contemporary international politics, and this political function determines the specific normative claims for the HRD. Current empirical conditions and agreements of international and supranational politics are the main framework that justifies the possible HRD claim and make such human rights feasible. However, this position seems compatible with the suggested argument for an individual right to voice.

3 Moral conceptions: bottom up

After the discussion of political conceptions in part 2, this part deals with moral conceptions and the several answers to the HRD-question they provide. Whereas the majority of political conceptions rejected the HRD, moving on to moral conceptions of human rights the amount of affirmations of the HRD claim rises. Authors of moral conceptions understand the HRD as an individual right rather than as a collective right to comprehensive political institutions. Thus, the demand for "democracy" in the HRD is usually concretized and narrowed down to a content that allows to be justified from a singular human standpoint. Inasmuch as collective, political normative aims such as a liberal democratic ethos or peace-building play a role in evaluating the HRD-question, their importance is linked to specific human needs, requirements for self-realization, capabilities or interests. Some authors who reject the comprehensive HRD nevertheless include minimal institutional claims such as a human right to participation or to specific democratic rights (such as the right to vote) in their reasoning. By this inclusion they show their support of the basic democratic principle of equal say that stays unchallenged in the moral conceptions. Turning to the two sub-categories of the moral conceptions, the intrinsic and the instrumental answers to the HRD question can be determined as follows:

(1) *Intrinsic moral conceptions* derive human rights from assumptions concerning human nature and general human capabilities and needs. It is postulated that they protect essential human features (such as particular understandings of human dignity) and foster the growth of individual potential and capabilities by guaranteeing basic rights and the satisfaction of basic needs. The line of reasoning of authors associated with this category usually begins with a discussion of moral rights and obligations. Some theorists using an intrinsic moral conception belong to the natural rights tradition. A successful intrinsic moral claim for an HRD must show that it is a right that each human has simply in virtue of being a human being. Democratic rights or institutions must have intrinsic value for maintaining a dignified human life.

(2) *Instrumental moral conceptions* argue, as do intrinsic moral conceptions, from the wellbeing and vulnerability of individuals. Disparaging of intrinsic moral conceptions, they emphasize the contingency of human rights due to their practical, historical, and political constructiveness. Human rights are seen as instruments to protect humans from injuries, which are defined as human rights violations referring to contemporary public reason, and the use of empirical knowledge. Characteristic of these accounts is a reference

to the principle of parsimony in dealing with essential, anthropological assumptions concerning human nature. This is to assert the culturally sensitive and politically correct universal applicability of human rights. A successful moral instrumental claim for an HRD must show that other human rights are thereby guaranteed or that political preconditions for a dignified life are secured.

At the center of intrinsic moral conceptions lies the attempt to prove the indispensability of an HRD from a substantial, individual perspective. Human rights are usually conceptualized as rights human beings have in virtue of being human. The claim that rights belong to each and every human being assumes the fundamental *principle of equality*. A closely related principle that is shared by most conceptions is the *principle of deference*. The principle of deference is understood to be a universal relation of recognition that likewise entitles and obligates individuals to respect and claim human rights and human dignity.[1]

The distinction between the two categories of moral rationales—intrinsic and instrumental—is not to be seen as sufficient but as heuristic, that is, helping to point out that the direction of argumentation is in each case different. For intrinsic conceptions, the study of human nature, human conditions, capabilities, and needs leads to (or does not lead to) the derivation of the HRD claim. Intrinsic moral conceptions understand human rights primarily as universal agency-, capability-, or interest-based *moral* rights. To mention some examples, James Griffin's *On Human Rights*[2] serves as a textbook example for a (normative) agency-based approach, just as Martha Nussbaum's book *Capabilities and Human Rightst*[3] does for a capabilities approach. In the footsteps of Habermasian, Seyla Benhabib endorses the HRD from a discourse-theoretic account while Rainer Forst develops a human rights understanding from the standpoint of one specific superior right, the basic right to justification. Carol C. Gould provides an alternative approach that tries to mediate between agency- and interest-based accounts by deriving a "social relational" human rights conception from a superior "theory of positive or effective freedom."[4] Moral instrumental

---

[1] Christoph Menke and Arnd Pollmann, *Philosophie der Menschenrechte* (Hamburg: Junius, 2007), 40.
[2] James Griffin, *On Human Rights* (Oxford: Oxford University Press, 2008).
[3] Martha C. Nussbaum, "Capabilities and Human Rights," 66(2) Fordham Law Review, (1997): 273–300.
[4] Carol C. Gould, "The Human Right to Democracy and Its Global Impact," in Cindy Holder and David Reidy (eds.), *Human Rights: The Hard Questions* (Cambridge: Cambridge University Press, 2013), 290–291.

conceptions try to prove the value of democracy by showing—often underpinned by empirical analysis—their utility for the protection of human interest that may or may not be derived from a particular intrinsic, moral conception of human nature but can also be established by referring to contemporary political consensus or to historical experience of injustices that call for institutional amendment.

3.1 Intrinsic moral conceptions

3.1.1 The human right to democracy is not a basic, but an applied human right (James Griffin)

According to James Griffin, the concept of human rights superseded the concept of natural right over the course of the Enlightenment. Criticizing a substantial indeterminacy of the contemporary concept of human rights, he tries to define them starting from the notions of *personhood* and *normative agency*. Personhood denotes the substantial content and values that go together with an understanding of the human being as a "functioning human agent". A functioning human agent is a person able to execute his normative agency. Human rights are defined as protections of normative agency, of the *differentia specifica* that enables persons, as *functioning human agents*, to develop and determine their own visions of a life worth living.[5] The three basic rights—*autonomy, liberty,* and *minimum provision*—serve as abstract measures to derive human rights. According to Griffin's distinction, autonomy is primarily understood as self-decision, self-rule or self-legislation. In contrast, liberty means having the inner and outer possibility to form and aim for the realization of one's particular concept of the good life. Minimum provision denotes the minimum of education, information and material resources that are necessary for the functioning human agent to have a real choice between several options daily life. *Personhood* and *practicalities* serve as the two conditions for the existence of a human right. To establish the existence of a universal human right, first it has to be shown that this right protects "an essential feature of the human standing." Second, it has to be shown that the determinate content of the right in question results from practical considerations (practicalities).[6] It might be unexpected to read that Griffin's liberal au-

---

5 Griffin, *On Human Rights*, 45.
   We reflect and assess. We form pictures of what a good life would be—often, it is true, only on small scale, but occasionally also on a large scale. And we try to realize these pictures. Homo sapiens can form and pursue conceptions of worthwhile life. Griffin, *On Human Rights*, 32
6 Griffin, *On Human Rights*, 43.

tonomy and liberty based account does not allow one to derive a universal human right to democratic participation in the strict sense. Griffin defines the right to democratic participation as an "applied human right" that can be legitimately claimed under contemporary conditions but cannot be consistently derived from the theoretical standpoint as a universal, basic human right:

> There are two kinds of derived rights: rights derived solely from fundamental ones, thus retaining universality, and rights derived by applying universal rights to particular conditions, not therefore universal. The human right to democratic participation, I want to say, is an applied right.[7]

According to Griffin, one major difficulty with the HRD claim is due to the fact that human rights and democracy have been historically developed to meet "quite different needs":

> Human rights grew up to protect what we see as constituting human dignity: the life, autonomy, and liberty of the individual. Democratic institutions grew up in our need for a decision procedure for groups—a procedure that is stable, manages transfer of power well, appropriate to a society whose members are more or less equal in power or worth, reconciles losers in social decisions to the basic structures of the society, and tends to promote the commonweal—that is, order, justice, security, and prosperity.[8]

The distinction between the directed collective goals of democracy and the protection function of human rights directed to the individual seems to explain at least part of the gap that Griffin identifies to exist between autonomy and democratic participation. The distinction between the individual level of human rights and the collective level of decisions for groups and the commonweal hinders Griffin to equate private autonomy and democratic participation. Formulating one's own conception of a worthwhile life, and making laws for everyone, expresses a potential contradiction between autonomy understood as self-legislation and public legislation that can stymie self-legislation.[9] Therefore, in a second step, Griffin tries to argue for an HRD by reference to the basic right of liberty, understood as the right to form and pursue one's own conception of a worthwhile life free from constraint from other actors, to a degree that is compatible with equal liberty for all.[10] But just "as one vote among millions will not protect one's actions from being stymied by public legislation," democratic partic-

---

7 Griffin, *On Human Rights*, 254.
8 Griffin, *On Human Rights*, 249.
9 Griffin, *On Human Rights*, 247.
10 Griffin, *On Human Rights*, ch. 9.

ipation does not seem to be a necessary condition of liberty, either.[11] Even though Griffin admits that democracy may be more likely than other forms of government to respect the domain of personhood, the inclusion of such a non-universal empirical premise would transgress his Spartan rational approach. Also, he is arguing that the requirement of fair political procedures cannot be derived from human rights alone.[12] After the rejection of a human right to democratic participation, Griffin discusses whether there is a weaker right to political (not necessarily democratic) participation. Objecting that a right to political participation can but need not protect anything valuable – if for example a biased ruler listens to the opinions but cannot fully understand or respond to it, the right to participation does not help to protect anything that is human rights relevant according Griffins conception: dignity and personhood.

> But a true human right must be in some way grounded in our human dignity—the dignity due to our personhood—and an entitlement merely to be listened to by a ruler who may be dismissive of one's views is hard to see in that light.[13]

Despite the conclusion that in the strict sense the rational, logical viewpoint does not allow the claim that human rights require democracy, Griffin admits for example strong empirical correlations such as the one between democratic governance and avoidance of famine. Reflecting about the complex modern conditions of society, he finally concludes that "human rights may require democracy in a weaker sense of 'require',"[14] and finally, "I am inclined to think, despite my inexpertise, that, in modern conditions, human rights do indeed require democracy."[15] Despite his belief that human rights to not encompass certain requirements of justice, fairness, and well-being, the empirical evidence, and the probability that a right to democracy can be morally justified because it ads forms of respect not yet included in human rights, leads him to a pragmatic ending: Responding to the question *Do human rights require democracy?*, he concludes: "Yes and No, depending upon circumstances."[16]

Griffin has been criticized for his conception of personhood that implies that only functioning human agents, i. e. capable and rational human beings, belong to the legal entity of human rights. Such criteria of capabilities and rationality

---

[11] Griffin, *On Human Rights*, 247.
[12] Griffin, *On Human Rights*, 242.
[13] Griffin, *On Human Rights*, 250.
[14] Griffin, *On Human Rights*, 248.
[15] Griffin, *On Human Rights*, 254.
[16] Griffin, *On Human Rights*, 255.

are not necessarily fulfilled, for example, by children, mentally incapacitated and handicapped persons. In a strict sense, these persons get excluded from the amount of so defined human beings and are thus also not entitled to claim "human" rights. Apart from this fundamental point of critique, Griffin's moral opposition to a HRD is logically consistent and unequivocal given the theoretical premises of his account. The practical, instrumental advantages of democracy compel him to end the chapter with a personal reservation against his own rejection of the HRD and with the partial affirmation of an HRD claim in modern conditions. Instrumental, consequentialist justifications of a human right to democracy thus prove to be intuitively vital even for the most hardcore rational moral philosophers. That the human right to democracy transcends a clear distinction between individual and collective dimension, between moral and political philosophical issues, as well as it transgresses the former sacrosanct *is–ought dichotomy*, seems inherent in the very nature of the debate. The practical, instrumental advantages of democracy for human wellbeing (the "is" aspects) are intuitively convincing even though the moral "ought" of an HRD is obviously difficult to derive from a strict moral theoretical viewpoint. The Griffin discussion shows that if human rights are strictly understood as protectors of human dignity, autonomy, and well-being, the intrinsic value of democratic participation must be shown apart from normative political, collective goals. Whereas this intrinsic value is questioned from Griffin, according to our next author, Martha Nussbaum, active political participation is required for the development of practical reason and thus counts as a substantial requirement for the development of individual capabilities.

3.1.2 Empowering human development instead of enacting a human right to democracy (Martha Nussbaum)

Shifting the attention from a modern Kantian approach to a neo-Aristotelian capabilities approach, the main focus in shifts to the question what basic conditions and (human) rights need to be guaranteed for an individual to develop his or her capabilities. The paradigmatic modern capability approach was designed from the Indian economist and philosopher Amartya Sen's. Arguing that in economic theory wellbeing must not only be measured by the factor of income, but must also include the criterion of what a human being needs for a good life. Martha Nussbaum, who closely worked together with Amartya Sen to further development of the capability approach, created a list of core capabilities, the so called "thick and vague conception of the good life" which can be summarized in a list of ten "human functioning capabilities".[17] Nussbaum's basic assumption is that the task of political arrangement cannot be understood, or performed well, without a "thicker" comprehensive theory of the human good than modern liberal theories provide. According to Nussbaum, we need an "intuitively powerful idea of truly human functioning that has roots in many different traditions and is independent of any particular metaphysical or religious view."[18] The primary task of politics is then to ensure that no citizen lacks in sustenance. Each and every human being has to be brought first across a threshold into a condition in which a truly human functioning can be lived, at least at a minimal level.[19] To outline a general structure of a human life, and to identify human ends across all areas and understandings of human life, Nussbaum designs a "thick vague conception of the good." She focuses on central "human functional capabilities" summarized under the following terms: 1. life, 2. bodily health, 3. bodily integrity, 4. sensation, imagination, thought, 5. emotions, 6. practical reason, 7. affiliation, 8. other species, 9. play, and 10. control over one's environment.[20] The central claim behind her list of functional capabilities is "that a life that lacks any one of these, no matter what else it has, will be regarded as seriously lacking in humanness."[21] According to Nussbaum, the core idea is that of the human as a dignified free being who shapes his or her own life in cooperation and reciprocity with others, rather than being passively shaped by the world like a "herd" animal.[22] She understands a life that is genuinely human as a life that is shaped *throughout* by human powers of practical reason and sociability, which leads her to include democratic claims such as "expressive and associational liberty" and "freedom of worship" in the list of requirements to enable the development of core capabilities.[23] Nussbaum conceives capabilities as having a close relationship to human rights. Preferring a "language of capa-

---

[17] Martha C. Nussbaum, *Woman and Human Development. The Capabilities Approach* (Cambridge: Cambridge University Press, 2000), 78–80.
[18] Martha C. Nussbaum, "Aristotelian Social Democracy," in Aristide Tessitore (ed.) *Aristotle and Modern Politics. The Persistence of Political Philosophy* (Notre Dame, Indiana: University of Notre Dame Press, 2002), 47–104, 53; Martha C. Nussbaum, *Woman and Human Development. The Capabilities Approach* (Cambridge: Cambridge University Press, 2000), 101.
[19] Nussbaum, "Aristotelian Social Democracy," 74–75.
[20] The central human functional capabilities are hereby listed in their slightly revised form, as given in Nussbaum, *Woman and Human Development*, 78–80. An earlier version can be found in Nussbaum, "Aristotelian Social Democracy," 62–73.
[21] Nussbaum, "Aristotelian Social Democracy," 71.
[22] Nussbaum, *Woman and Human Development*, 72.
[23] Nussbaum, *Woman and Human Development*, 72.

bilities" to a "language of rights," she suggests that the language of human rights should remain close to the ethical role of basic capabilities, "in the sense that the justification for saying that people have such natural rights usually proceeds by pointing to some capability-like feature of persons (rationality, language) that they actually have on at least a rudimentary level."[24]

Nussbaum's famous article "Aristotelian Social Democracy,"[25] which introduced her essentialist capabilities approach, along with her concept of a "thick vague conception of the good," precedes the core HRD debate as evaluated by Cohen onwards. Combining Aristotelian and selected liberal insights, she originally intended to provide the philosophical basis for a particular form of social democracy.[26] Her approach was further elaborated and—with an eye to political philosophical questions—slightly modified in *Woman and Human Development: The Capabilities Approach*. Although it is not explicitly linked to the HRD debate, I include her capabilities approach because it paradigmatically represents a highly influential "species of a human rights approach"[27], and because her list of central human functional capabilities includes practical reason, affiliation, and (political and material) control over one's environment, which lead her to particular claims for democratic rights such as the right of political participation, the protection of free speech and for association.[28] The connection to the HRD debate is further revealed insofar as the political liberties not only play an instrumental role in preventing material disaster (as was shown by Amartya Sen)[29], but that they are in Nussbaum's view valuable in their own right.[30] For political purposes, where adult citizens are concerned securing "capability, not functioning, is the appropriate political goal" because "citizens have to be left free to determine their own course" in respect to their potential functioning. [31]

Social-democratic ideals thus underlie Nussbaum's universal political goals, as well as her thesis that political change is based on a bottom-up recognition process that is both enacted and driven by individuals and constitutive of peoples. Despite the hope that the capabilities list will "steer the process of global-

---

24 Nussbaum, *Woman and Human Development*, 100.
25 Nussbaum, "Aristotelian Social Democracy."
26 Nussbaum, "Aristotelian Social Democracy," 47.
27 Martha C. Nussbaum, "Capabilities and Human Rights," 20 *Harvard Human Rights Journal* (2007): 22.
28 Nussbaum, *Woman and Human Development*, 78 ff.
29 In the Introduction to *Woman and Human Development*, Nussbaum explains the relation between Sen's and her own understanding of the capabilities approach. (Nussbaum, *Woman and Human Development*, at 11–15.) I will return to Sen's approach in the following section.
30 Nussbaum, *Woman and Human Development*, 96.
31 Nussbaum, *Woman and Human Development*, 87.

ization, giving it a rich set of human goals and a vivid sense of human waste and tragedy," its realization will be contingent on a functioning social and procedural relation between citizens and nation states:

> Nonetheless, even a highly moralized globalism needs nation states at its core, because transnational structures (...) are insufficiently accountable to citizens and insufficiently representative of them. Thus the primary role for the capabilities account remains that of providing political principles that can underlie national constitutions; and this means that practical implementation must remain to a large extent the job of citizens in each nation.[32]

Approaching Rawls's conception of public reason, and the related process of reaching a reflective equilibrium with an eye to international relations, Nussbaum reminds us of the fundamental importance of the nation state, as well as the long process of reaching any transnational consensus on the capabilities list. Whereas consensus about certain elements on the list already exists, an effective pursuit of many of the items on the list requires far greater international cooperation among nations.[33] Although social, as well as liberal democratic, ideas of a just society clearly supply a background *telos* to Nussbaum's approach, her commitment to civil and political democratic liberties, along with her profound understanding of human development processes, seems to be the reason why she refuses to claim a prescribed universal top-down HRD. For Nussbaum, encouraging consensus in a Rawlsian growth-minded manner is done by fostering soft power and development aid in order to promote capabilities, rather than by the implementation of any straightforward human rights legislation. Finally, her strong commitment to universal validity of the capabilities approach is supported by five arguments:

> First, *multiple realizability:* each of the capabilities may be concretely realized in a variety of different ways, in accordance with individual tastes, local circumstances, and traditions. Second, *capability as a goal:* the basic political principles focus on promoting capabilities, not actual functioning, in order to leave citizens the choice whether to pursue the relevant function or not to pursue it. Third, *liberties and practical reasons:* the content of the capabilities list gives a central role to citizens' powers of choice and to traditional political and civil liberties. Fourth, *political liberalism:* the approach is intended as the moral core of a specifically political conception, and the object of a political overlapping consensus among people who have otherwise very different comprehensive views of the good. Fifth, *constraints on implementation:* the approach is designed to offer the philosophical grounding for constitutional principles, but the implementation of such principles must be left, for the most part, to the internal politics of the nation in question, although international agen-

---

[32] Nussbaum, *Woman and Human Development*, 105.
[33] Nussbaum, *Woman and Human Development*, 103–105.

cies and other governments are justified in using persuasion—and in especially grave cases economic or political sanctions—to promote such developments.[34]

Nussbaum's comprehensive approach explicitly addresses individual, social, national, and international interdependencies and conditions that shape human development processes. She links a distinct moral philosophical, essentialist standpoint to a Rawlsian political conception of human rights. The approach has proved an inspiring base for human rights thinkers who aim to bridge the gap between anthropological, social and political focuses. [35]

3.1.3 The universal value of democracy (Amartya Sen)

Amartya Sen, the "inventor" of the modern capabilities approach in human rights theory, represents a slightly different version of the capabilities approach compared to Nussbaum's. Sen is stressing that human rights and capabilities are not to be seen as congruent. Whereas many human rights "can be seen as rights to particular capabilities" others, like human rights to important process freedoms, "cannot be adequately analyzed within the capability framework";[36] "Capabilities and the opportunity aspect of freedom, important as they are, have to be supplemented by considerations of fair processes and the lack of violation of people's right to invoke and utilise them."[37] Sen criticizes Nussbaum's lack of

---

34 Seyla Benhabib criticizes the close relation Nussbaum claims to exist between human capabilities and rights:

Nussbaum envisages a one-to-one correspondence between a philosophically derived list of human rights, based upon a moral theory of capabilities, and the enactments of specific legislatures. She thereby neglects how legitimate variations in the interpretations, contextualization and application of human rights can emerge across self-governing polities. Seyla Benhabib, "Is There a Human Right to Democracy? Beyond Interventionism and Indifference," in Christoph Broszies and Henning Hahn (eds.): Philosophical Dimensions of Human Rights. Some Contemporary Views (Dordrecht/Heidelberg/London/New York: Springer) 201.

35 Benhabib, "Is There a Human Right to Democracy? Beyond Interventionism and Indifference," 201.

36 Amartya Sen, "Human Rights and Capabilities," 6(2) Journal of Human Development (2005): 151.

37 Sen, "Human Rights and Capabilities," 157. See also Amartya Sen, "Elements of a Theory of Human Rights," 32(4) Philosophy & Public Affairs (2004): 315–356, 336:

Although the idea of capability has considerable merit in the assessment of the opportunity aspect of freedom, it cannot possibly deal adequately with the process aspect of freedom, since capabilities are characteristics of individual advantages, and they fall short of telling us enough

distinction between rights understood as moral principles compared to rights understood as legal entitlements that would lead to a "canonical list" how it could not be chosen without further specification of content. But such a specification would involve a substantive diminution of the domain of public reason.[38] Sen considers public reason to be the legitimate source where process freedoms and related human rights are discussed and established. Earlier, Sen stipulated democracy to be a universal value, citing intrinsic, instrumental and constructive reasons:

> Viewed in this light, the merits of democracy and its claim as a universal value can be related to certain distinct virtues that go with its unfettered practice. Indeed, we can distinguish three different ways in which democracy enriches the lives of the citizens. First, political freedom is a part of human freedom in general, and exercising civil and political rights is a crucial part of good lives of individuals as social beings. Political and social participation has intrinsic value for human life and well-being. To be prevented from participation in the political life of the community is a major deprivation. Second, as I have just discussed (in disputing the claim that democracy is in tension with economic development), democracy has an important instrumental value in enhancing the hearing that people get in expressing and supporting their claims to political attention (including claims of economic needs). Third—and this is a point to be explored further—the practice of democracy gives citizens an opportunity to learn from one another, and helps society to form its values and priorities. Even the idea of "needs", including the understanding of "economic needs," requires public discussion and exchange of information, views, and analyses. In this sense, democracy has constructive importance, in addition to its intrinsic value for the lives of the citizens and its instrumental importance in political decisions. The claims of democracy as a universal value have to take note of this diversity of considerations.[39]

First, Sen posits the intrinsic value of political and social participation as an essential part of human life and well-being. Human freedom is defined as an indispensable part of a self-realizing existence. The lack of political freedom as a part of this human freedom is considered a major deprivation. Sen explicitly claims civil and political *freedom* to be crucial for the good life, and the right to political participation to be vital. Freedom is valued "for the substantive opportunity it gives to the pursuit of our objectives and goals."[40] As further elaborated in *Rationality and Freedom* and by reference to social choice theory, Sen advocates

---

about the fairness or equity of the processes involved, or about the freedom of citizens to invoke and utilize procedures that are equitable.

38 Benhabib, "Interventionism and Indifference," ch. 10.3; Amartya Sen, *Rationality and Freedom* (Cambridge, MA: Harvard University Press, 2002), 333–334.
39 Amartya Sen, "Democracy as a Universal Value," 10(3) Journal of Democracy (1999): 10.
40 Sen, *Rationality and Freedom*.

the thesis of a reciprocal relationship between rationality and freedom. The assessment of freedom requires a person's reasoned preferences and valuations; whereas rationality depends on freedom of thought.[41] The second argument emphasizes the instrumental value democracies can have in strengthening hearing and political attention for the claims of the citizens. The more elaborate the democratic procedures are, the more should they allow an effective interest representation. Additionally, democracy proofs an educational function. If the citizens have to practice democracy, they gain democratic competences. The processes of active deliberation, public opinion-making and particular interest representation lead to the citizens' formation of priorities and values, and to an exchange of information that potentially rises the recognition of diversity. The deliberative impact Sen points out as an intrinsic value of democracy is further elaborated by the following two authors who are both representatives of contemporary Critical Theory: Rainer Forst and Seyla Benhabib.

3.1.4 The right to justification as a right to democratic procedures (Rainer Forst)

In the tradition of Critical Theory, Rainer Forst presents a constructivist conception of human rights. In his outstanding article "The Basic Right to Justification: Toward a Constructivist Conception of Human Rights" he shows the right to justification to be the origin of any legitimate human rights claim. The article predates the publication of Cohen's article (and thus also the main HRD debate) but is nonetheless indispensable for the HRD discussion of human rights. Forst's approach is informed by a confrontation with some of the basic objections that have been brought against conceptions of universal human rights, such as the problem of cultural relativity, and of Western, capitalist domination over other societies ("neocolonialism"). The objection that human rights are a historical project of Western states leads to the conclusion that their normative validity can hardly be promoted as "universal"; rather, they must be seen as culturally and politically relative. The further objection that "Western" human rights are a tool used to dominate non-Western societies also casts doubt on the political interpretation and application of human rights.[42] Taking these concerns seriously, Forst aims to provide a conception of human rights "that is culturally sensi-

---

41 Sen, *Rationality and Freedom*, 5.
42 Rainer Forst, "The Basic Right to Justification: Toward a Constructivist Conception of Human Rights," 6(1) *Constellations* (1999): 35.

tive as it is culturally neutral—a conception that proves to be interculturally non-rejectionable, universally valid, and applicable in particular cases."[43] Assuming that a proper examination of the relevant *intra*-cultural discourses is a proviso for an *inter*-cultural discussion about human rights, Forst argues for a *basic right to justification* to be the minimal normative core from which such a conception should be derived.[44] The right to justification is understood as a kind of reciprocal and general aspiration that is undeniable and can be demanded. It is a basic moral right in the sense that it itself need not be a specific, intersubjectively grounded, and practically accepted human right, but rather the basic condition for deriving concrete rights. The right to justification expresses the most general and basic claim of human beings to be respected as autonomous moral persons, at least in the sense that one cannot treat them without also giving them an adequate reason for the way they are being treated. On this conception, the integrity of individual members of a society is closely interlinked with the integrity of the society as a whole. Respecting the sanctity of personal integrity within a society, and the cultural integrity of the whole—and understanding it to be an autonomously grown cultural structure with a particular self-understanding—leads the way to the (subordinate) normative claim of political self-determination.[45]

> "Integrity" is an appropriate term in this context, since it implies that the culture in question is a self-understanding and, in a certain sense, "complete" unity, as well as a sense-bearing, quasi-organic whole that meets certain standards of genuineness and respectability. The culture is, so to speak, a fully integrated unity full of integrity. On this basis, every single external encroachment can be regarded as a violation of this integrity that forces the culture to compromise its values and thereby its authenticity. The imposition of an "external" morality of human rights is thus considered to be such an encroachment.[46]

From the high value of integrity it follows that every social-cultural structure and its moral legitimacy depend on the members recognition of the reciprocal and

---

[43] Forst, "The Basic Right to Justification: Toward a Constructivist Conception of Human Rights", 36.
[44] Forst, "The Basic Right to Justification: Toward a Constructivist Conception of Human Rights", 36.
[45] Forst, "The Basic Right to Justification: Toward a Constructivist Conception of Human Rights", 37–38: "What is more, *the claim to be a respectable, fully integrated unity full of integrity depends on the claim that otherwise the integrity of the members of this culture would suffer.*" (Emphasis added.)
[46] Forst, "The Basic Right to Justification: Toward a Constructivist Conception of Human Rights", 37–38

hermeneutical processes between themselves and the society as a whole. If the recognition on one side is challenged, the questioning must be accounted for by reasons, not by force. Human rights thus spring from the human demand for reasons, for the justification of certain rules, laws, and institutions, where the reasons people have already been given are no longer convincing.[47] The demand for human rights arises from the members' *experience of injustice* within the culture; the language of human rights becomes the language of *social emancipation*.[48] As Forst points out, rights do not come from an authoritative source (such as the state, a divine power, or nature), but are a collective project of a sovereign political community:

> Thus a political community is to be regarded as "sovereign" in the sense that its members regard it as a collective project of establishing just institutions founded on the citizens' recognition of one another as persons with the right to justification. . . . Rights are not "granted" vertically by a state, but instead are accepted and conferred horizontally in processes of justification, and thus are an expression of mutual recognition.[49]

Human rights and the sovereignty of a political community are considered to be equally primordial. The justified establishment of a basic social structure leads to a democratic state of law in which "the citizens are subjects of political justification as citizens" as well as "the subjects of law as legal persons."[50] Forst's general conception of human rights, justified in a discursive theory of moral constructivism that represents "the normative center of a plurality of possible politically constructivist concrete interpretations" is thus distinctively aimed to establish a more just social order—"one that actually justifies itself to those who are its subjects."[51]

The distinction between the core moral right of justification and the concrete, legal human right sets apart the moral and the legal dimensions of human rights. However, the concrete process of establishing universal human

---

[47] Forst, "The Basic Right to Justification: Toward a Constructivist Conception of Human Rights", 40: "In such a situation of internal conflicts there arises—not necessarily, but under certain conditions and in our day as a rule—the demand for *human rights:* it arises 'from within', and is directed to something 'internal'." (Emphasis added)
[48] Forst, "The Basic Right to Justification: Toward a Constructivist Conception of Human Rights", 41–42.
[49] Forst, "The Basic Right to Justification: Toward a Constructivist Conception of Human Rights", 49.
[50] Forst, "The Basic Right to Justification: Toward a Constructivist Conception of Human Rights", 50.
[51] Forst, "The Basic Right to Justification: Toward a Constructivist Conception of Human Rights", 56.

rights from the bottom up, originating from local communities, would seem to necessitate the direct involvement and political recognition of human rights in a globally realized inquiry. Human rights could only be "universal" if they fall into a globally shared intersection of human rights claims. The fact that the justification and democratization processes have been historically nonuniform over the face of the earth raises considerable difficulties for Forst's theory. Guaranteeing the human right to justification (as a variant of the human right to democracy) is, on the one hand, the prerequisite for a political community to discuss and claim human rights. On the other hand, such an "authoritarian" imposition of the human right to justification must be post facto. Forst tries to solve this conflict in *Towards a Critical Theory of Transnational Justice* by proposing a *principle of minimal transnational justice*:

> To break the vicious circle of multiple, internal and external domination and to establish a *political autonomy both within particular states and within the international system*, a principle of *minimal transnational justice* is called for. According to this principle, members of societies of multiple domination have a legitimate claim to the resources necessary to establish a (minimally) justified democratic order within their political community *and* that this community be a participant of (roughly) equal standing in the global economic and political system.[52]

The principle of minimal transnational justice seems to put the international community in charge to realize minimal democratic conditions in all member states.[53] However, this authorization can only be legitimate as long as the international community stays accountable and provides justified reasons for its actions to the members.

If we understand and summarize Forst's right to justification as a human right to democracy claim, it's one that gets his particular justification out of the intersubjective nature of the human being. The right to justification thus represents the human need to ask for and provide reasons, to be heard and involved

---

52 Rainer Forst, "Toward a Critical Theory of Transnational Justice," 32(1–2) *Metaphilosophy* (2001): 174. (Original Emphasis)
53 Forst, "Toward a Critical Theory of Transnational Justice", 175–176:
 Whether the institutionalization of minimal justice and the results of justificatory discourse on the basis will lead to a federation of states in a subsidiary "world republic" or to something like a "world state" is hard to predict and not to be predetermined; it is a matter of the kind of institutions that are seen to be necessary to fulfill the demands of justice. Still, the realization of the minimum already presupposes a much higher degree of institutionalization than the present one, both for safeguarding the social minimum within states and for establishing (roughly) equal standing between states.

in the social of political community one is living in. As for a just society the successful communication between individual and public sphere is crucial, the responsibility for the basic right to justification is on both, the individual and the political actors level.

3.1.5 Legitimate political decision-making depends on democratic self-government (Seyla Benhabib)

Alike Forst, Seyla Benhabib can be associated with the critical theory tradition. Her focus on the the discourse-theoretical model and the idea of freedom of communication of Jürgen Habermas is more explicitly pronounced in comparison to Forst's thinking. For Benhabib, the normative core principle of human rights is Hannah Arendt's claim of "the right to have rights." Pointing to phenomenological conditions of human existence, Benhabib shows that the relation to the other is guided by the norms of *equal worth* and *complementary reciprocity*.[54] She thus extends Arendt's "right to have rights" to a principally political "right to membership in a political community" by proposing a non-state-centered conception of the right to have rights. She understands the latter as "the claim of each human person to be recognized and to be protected as a legal personality by the world community."[55] The justification of human rights is considered to be a dialogical procedure taking place under the premise that the recognition of *your* right to have rights serves as a proviso that enables you to accept or reject *my* rights claims.[56] Benhabib enforces the claim that human rights have to become transmitted into legal rights. Human rights are moral principles that are reliant on becoming embedded into a democratic system of legal norms bridging the "gap between moral and justice."[57] Self-determination is a fundamental human-rights-claim indispensable for interpretation and discourse: "My thesis," explains Benhabib, "is that without the right to self-government, which is exercised through proper legal and political channels, we cannot justify the range of variation in the content of basic human rights as being legitimate."[58]

Democratic legitimacy and diversity spring from the normative principles of justification that bear fruit under the condition of self-determination. "Integrity" and "democratic itineration," which continuously improve the process of discur-

---

54 Benhabib, "Interventionism and Indifference," 197.
55 Benhabib, "Interventionism and Indifference," 195.
56 Benhabib, "Interventionism and Indifference," 195 ff.
57 Benhabib, "Interventionism and Indifference," 196, 206.
58 Benhabib, "Interventionism and Indifference," 207.

sive justification, are concepts of importance comparable to the conception of the basic right to justification in Forst. After following Habermas's thesis that the principle of democracy should establish a procedure of legitimate law-making, and that the principle is based on the condition that only those "statutes may claim legitimacy that can meet with the assent (*Zustimmung*) of all citizens in a discursive process of legislation which has been legally constituted."[59] Benhabib insists on the claim that the rhetoric of interventions should become clearly distinguished from the human rights discourse. Whereas political ethics must be concerned with the weighing of intentions and consequences, of responsibility and dispositional ethics, the moral philosophical fundamental debate about the philosophical justification of human rights and its directive, awareness-raising function should not be devalued by obvious difficulties hindering the implementation of the theoretical claims in international relations.[60]

Forst and Benhabib are committed to the discourse-theoretical approach that takes democratic values and the procedural advantages of democratic law and governmental structures to be the only adequate context of a just society characterized by a vivid culture of reciprocal justification and recognition. Both authors are attentive to the need for a clear distinction between moral and political dimensions of human rights. However, there are unanswered questions concerning the concrete realization of a critical theory of transnational justice or of the universal claim for the right of justification. The structural weakness identified by Brunkhorst in Hannah Arendt's claim of the right to have rights comes up again: the fundamental normative rights (rights of justification / right to have rights) are moral philosophical settlements lacking democratic legitimacy. The "worldwide civil right to have civil rights" requires a federal, republican political system.[61] Such a presupposition necessarily also reduces the

---

59 Benhabib, "Interventionism and Indifference," 208.
60 Nevertheless, as Kant observed, there is a distinction between a "political moralist," who misuses moral principles to justify political decisions, and a "moral politician," who tries to remain true to moral principles in shaping political events. The discourse of human rights has often been exploited and misused by "political moralists"; its proper place is to guide moral politicians, be they citizens or leaders. All that we can offer as philosophers is a clarification of what we can regard as legitimate and just in the domain of human rights themselves. Benhabib, "Interventionism and Indifference," 212.
61 Carol Gould referred to the problem by calling it "the constitutional circle." She identifies the problem that rights agreed to in a democratic process of constitution making would already have to be constrained by rights. Constructively interpreting the circularity, she suggests the evidence for primary "constitutional" claims to be experiental or phenomenological as it presents itself to us in the structures of everyday action Philosophy of Psychiatry and social interaction: What reveals these rights, practically speaking, is the daily and recurrent recognition by individuals of

pluralism of human life forms and cultural diversity, which gives the fundamental rights claim an absolutist note. However, Benhabib counters the reproach by pointing to the hermeneutical (circular) structure of practical reason:

> [W]e always already have to assume *some understanding* of equality, reciprocity and symmetry in order to be able to frame the discourse model in the first place, but each of these normative terms are then open to reflexive justification or recursive validation within the discourse itself. Such "recursive validation" of the preconditions of discourse has been misunderstood by many as indicating a vicious circle. I disagree with these claims which often ignore the "hermeneutical structure" of practical reason and wish to have practical reason proceed as if it were theoretical reason—that is, from uncontested first premises.[62]

By simply admitting that, from a logical perspective, a first (non-democratical) positing of basic values foregoes every democratic validation, moral criteria for such positing become relevant. Benhabib shifts the attention to the utmost necessity that human rights be defined and legitimized through their political function of guaranteeing fundamental rights (such as the right to have rights) *to the individual*, rather than their function of providing reasons for interference by international authorities. The condition that human rights values have to be confirmed by public reasoning (even if this is sometimes only retroactively possible) sets an example in underlining the conviction that the Western (power) political human rights setting in the longer term should recede in support of social, deliberative recognition criteria and processes. Human rights are first of all meant to clear up unjust social, cultural, and political life conditions that are legitimately identified from the perspective of affected individuals themselves. The

---

others as being like themselves, namely, as agents with claims to the conditions for their self-developing or self-transformative activity. This recognition characteristically takes place in several ways: first, in the basic reciprocity in which individuals make claims on one another to be free from harm and from constraints on their actions; and in exchange grant this same recognition of negative freedom and equality to the others; or else expect a benefit in return for benefit done. This level of instrumental or tit-for-tat reciprocity acknowledges the right of the other by virtue of an assertion of the reciprocal validity of one's own claim; that is, in asserting one's own right, one acknowledges the validity of the other's claim as a right by virtue of reciprocally recognizing it as like one's own. Beyond this minimal reciprocity, a more socialized recognition of the other as having rights develops in the context of shared activity with others in pursuit of commonly agreed-upon ends. Where there is social agency or cooperation required in joint activity oriented toward common goals, the reciprocity is one of mutual recognition of those common rights that apply to such cooperative activity – notably, rights of participation in the determination of common goals and of the process of achieving them. Carol C. Gould, *Globalizing Democracy and Human Rights* (Cambridge: Cambridge University Press, 2004), 41.
See also Gould, "Global Impact," 286.
62 Benhabib, "Interventionism and Indifference," 198–199.

public reasoning has to integrate the views of different individuals who are experiencing and reflecting about social reality, and who are learning to form or adopt the perspective of a general moral standpoint.

3.1.6 The human right to democracy as the capstone of international law (Stephan Kirste)

In his "Human Right to Democracy as the Capstone of Law," Stephan Kirste aims to provide a reconstruction of law on the basis of freedom. Understanding freedom as the highest moral value and as the normative benchmark to evaluate moral human rights claims, he supports the HRD claim. According to Kirste, the individual right to active participation secures legal freedom, which is why the HRD is defined as the capstone of international law.

In the tradition of critical theory, Kirste conceptualizes the HRD as "a right to participate in the deliberating, decision-making and interpreting procedures of general rights and duties."[63] He argues that the HRD has to be justified by a common principle of human rights and democracy, namely the principle of legal freedom. Taking self-determination as the modern understanding of freedom, he distinguishes between negative freedom (i.e. the independence of the self from heteronomy) and positive freedom (i.e. the ability of the self to determine the motives of its action).[64] Legal freedom is secured if legal norms provide for individual rights. Only through the attribution of individual rights (and, in the global context, of human rights), the human being is transformed into a legal person, an autonomous subject. Thus, legal freedom is seen as "the possibility for a person to determine his or her own actions not being subjected to any other person."[65] Reviewing several positions about the human right to democracy, Kirste assumes it is generally accepted that human persons should not only enjoy freedom, but also decide about their liberties. Referring to Georg Jellinek's use of the Hegelian concept of the *status activus*, Kirste argues for democratic participation as an end in itself, ensuring the political autonomy of the individual:

> Without negative human rights law is self-contradictory, since it is necessarily directed towards freedom: without active human rights in the *status activus*, the catalogue of human rights is incomplete. Both are necessary and sufficient conditions for the reconstruction of

---

63 Kirste, "The Human Right to Democracy as a Capstone of Law," 17.
64 Kirste, "The Human Right to Democracy as a Capstone of Law," 13.
65 Kirste, "The Human Right to Democracy as a Capstone of Law," 13.

law on the basis of freedom. The active status of political autonomy as the basis of a right to democracy then rounds up the legal status.[66]

Because of the reflexive structure of law, the HRD is not seen as a "right that the legal order paternalistically grants the people as this would mean granting and withholding the right to democracy at the same time":

> People rather realize the right to democracy in the foundation of the legal order itself—be it guaranteed by a national, supranational or international legal order and be it united in an explicit right to democracy or be it a unifying principle for a couple of rights securing aspects of it.[67]

Kirste understands human rights as intrinsic to the international law, its organization and democratic legitimation. He claims that the human right to democracy is the capstone of the concretization of the potential of freedom in the concept of law.[68] Kirste replaces the Habermasian conception of co-originality of human rights and democracy with a justification of the intrinsic coherence between human rights and democracy based on law as an order of freedom.[69] The human right to democracy is not primarily a positive right to democratic institutions or a negative right to be protected from political domination; it is primarily the authorization of the individual participant to involve him- or herself into the political process, to be a part of the community that not only adapts but co-determine rights and duties:

> A particular legal order that does not only protect and limit freedom, but in which the enactment of its norms is organized in a way that the individual takes part in it, builds the complete structure of law on freedom.[70]

The right to participate in the political process of one's community becomes the condition of the self-realization of individual freedom. The HRD constrains the realization of human rights *in actu*, because it empowers the right-holders not just to claim but also to actively create, revise, and execute human rights: "The demos is the demiurgos of its legal identity."[71]

---

66 Kirste, "The Human Right to Democracy as a Capstone of Law," 15.
67 Kirste, "The Human Right to Democracy as a Capstone of Law," 17.
68 Kirste, "The Human Right to Democracy as a Capstone of Law," 17.
69 Kirste, "The Human Right to Democracy as a Capstone of Law," 2.
70 Kirste, "The Human Right to Democracy as a Capstone of Law," 16.
71 Kirste, "The Human Right to Democracy as a Capstone of Law," 18.

3.1.7 Social democracy as a global vision (Carol C. Gould)

In both her book, *Globalizing Democracy and Human Rights*, and in an article "The Human Right to Democracy and its Global Impact," Carol C. Gould presents a comprehensive approach that argues in favor of an HRD against the background of a broad, substantial conception of social democracy. She is particularly concerned with the question of what the universal demand and recognition of an HRD would imply for global governance. She begins with considering the main objections against an HRD brought up by Cohen and other authors in the Rawlsian tradition: (i) an HRD would require an unrealistic obligation to enforce it by means of international interventions; (ii) it would violate the premier human right to self-determination, and thus is not sufficiently tolerant towards decent societies; (iii) the HRD involves "a Western or liberal imposition on societies organized around a common good or social harmony conception"; and (iv) democracy requires equality, which is a too demanding a request for some societies, and exceeds a minimal list of human rights.[72]

To the first two objections Gould replies that no direct connection between recognizing and criticizing human rights violation, and intervening to stop such violations, must be postulated. It is a separate question what measures should be taken to help people recover their human rights. Further it has to be asked what would be involved in putting institutions in place to fulfill these human rights.[73] The recognition of democratic participation as a human right entails neither a right nor a duty to establish democracy globally through forceful intervention, for the functions of human rights, prior to any interventions, are normative and moral functions of serving as goals for the development of institutions and as a basis for social and political critique and change.[74] Gould's broader "social and relational" conception of democracy exceeds electoral democracy and does not call for a particular governmental structure. Her social and relational approach is mainly defined through its reference to a concept of people's agency as emerging through social practices, including practices of reciprocity.[75] Gould's crucial assumptions concern the (universal) request standing behind the idea of human rights which should identify and realize "the material, social and political conditions needed for the development of people's agency, where this agency is taken in the first place as human life activity and in a fuller sense as the

---

72 Gould, "Global Impact," 285–286.
73 Gould, "Global Impact," 287.
74 Gould, "Global Impact," 288.
75 Gould, "Global Impact," 290.

development of capacities and the realization of long term projects over time."[76] Indirectly replying to objection (iii) above, i.e. the criticism that an HRD would be a Western imposition, Gould refers to universal human conditions and the potential of a conception to mediate between agency-, capability-, and interest-based accounts. A human rights conception thus always implies a certain amount of shared values. However, this by no means implies that a common good or social harmony conception has to be implemented; her conception of justice as equal positive freedom promotes equality rights to the *conditions of self-transformation*.[77]

Responding to Cohen's equality-objection—(iv) democracy requires equality, which is a too demanding request for some societies, and exceeds a minimal list of human rights—Gould convincingly points out that human rights entail a strong commitment to equality, "perhaps even a stronger one than democracy does, or at least a more universal egalitarian commitment."[78] Gould distinguishes her conception of agency from Griffin's Kantian agency conception by a stronger emphasis on the social and relational needs. In contrast to Griffin's emphasis on terms of human dignity or on a reference to a "high-level-purposiveness" of the person, Gould takes social and relational needs as primary criteria for normative reasoning.[79] The equal basic agency of all social beings leads to the requirement of access to conditions for people to develop capacities and realize projects.[80] Proceeding from an "account of positive or effective freedom" that views people as equal agents, Gould points out the correlative distinction that exists between "basic agency (whether in individual or social forms) and its development" and "basic human rights (as conditions for any human activity and non-basic (though still essential) human rights, which are conditions needed for people's fuller flourishing."[81] Further, Gould sees her account as closely related to the capability approaches but "without giving exclusive weight to these capabilities to the neglect of the fundamental capacity to choose, on the one hand, or of the realization of long-term projects, on the other."[82] It is crucial to pay attention to social practices in order to understand Gould's overall conception:

---

76 Gould, "Global Impact," 290.
77 Gould, "Global Impact," 291.
78 Gould, "Global Impact," 288.
79 Gould, "Global Impact," 290.
80 Gould, "Global Impact," 291.
81 Carol C. Gould, "The Human Right to Democracy," 290.
82 Gould, "The Human Right to Democracy," 290.

I suggest that the relevant practices that lay the ground for the acceptance of human rights are more elementary ones, evident in both interpersonal and institutional contexts. They involve the practices of reciprocal recognition found in everyday experience, in which people implicitly or explicitly recognize the equal agency of others. These practices include not only the fundamental forms of communicative interactions, which Habermas has emphasized, but also the range of non-verbal interactions through which people reciprocally recognize each other, e.g., in ordinary greetings, or in Goffman-type "vehicular interactions"; in which people reciprocally navigate their encounters with others, whether as pedestrians or drivers.[83]

Human rights specify the conditions such as "absence of constraints such as threats to bodily security, or restriction on basic liberty (including freedom from domination)", availability of enabling material and social conditions (such as means of subsistence, health-care, education, support for crucial social relationships etc.), and various democratic rights such as freedom of expression and association.[84] Apart from these instrumental arguments for democracy, the argument of democracy should itself be seen as a human right:

Various democratic rights—e.g., freedom of expression and association—play an important role in protecting people's basic liberty and also their further flourishing. But beyond this, we can see the argument for democracy as itself a human right. Inasmuch as people are social beings, or what I have called "individuals-in-relations": engaging in common or joint activities with others can be seen as itself one of the prime conditions for their freedom. Common activities are here broadly understood to be activities oriented to shared goals. If none are to dominate others in these joint activities, they must have equal rights to participate in determining their course.[85]

Democracy is thus seen as a normative form of decision-making that involves equal rights of participation among the members of any given community. Gould's expansive conception of democracy "supports the extension of democratic forms of decision-making to institutions beyond the political."[86] Such an extension of democratic forms of decision-making could be installed f.e. in economic firms through the requirement for workers' self-management (work-place democracy). In several social, cultural and political areas, the democratic ethos should be actively cultivated. The particular understanding of democracy must be "social and relational" in a way that it supports to cultivate intersubjective and cooperative human relationships. By this, the superior goal of individual

---

83 Gould, "The Human Right to Democracy," 291.
84 Gould, "The Human Right to Democracy," 291–292.
85 Gould, "The Human Right to Democracy," 292.
86 Gould, "The Human Right to Democracy," 292.

and social self-transformation understood as positive freedom within his social, cultural and political can become realized in society. The understanding of substantial democracy and human rights is complemented by a cross-border reflection. Gould explains the additional need for new forms of global democratic participation by the impacts that decisions and policies of institutions of global governance and other powerful actors like nation states and corporations have on people "who are distantly situated and not part of these institutions or communities."[87] Applying the two criteria for justifying democratic participation and deliberation and for determining their scope at domestic level—the common activity principle and the all-affected principle[88]—Gould suggests that affected people (in terms of an appeal to the fulfillment of basic human rights) should have significant input into the decision or policy in question, though not necessarily fully equal rights of participation:

> Perhaps we could specify "all affected" as "those importantly affected" or perhaps "relevantly affected." Yet another direction would be to add to the idea of joint activity a conception of common interests and shared needs. We could then argue that not only those who belong to an institutional framework have rights of democratic participation, but so do those who have common interests in the particular course of action or the policy under consideration, even if they are not participants in the activity itself.[89]

---

[87] Gould, "The Human Right to Democracy," 292–293.

[88] According to Gould, justice has the normative priority over the requirements of democracy. Justice may legitimately constrain the democratic process when it leads to outcomes that violate individuals' right to equal freedom. Thus, two principles to justify democracy as a substantial conception are given: the *common activities* and the *all-affected criterion*. The first criterion appeals to rights of democratic participation among the members of a political community.

[People are] individuals-in-relations, ... engaging in common or joint activities with others can be seen as itself one of the prime conditions for their freedom. Common activities are here broadly understood tobe activities oriented to shared goals. If none are to dominate others in these joint activities, they must have equal rights to participate in determining their course. This is a very general principle that pertains to joint activities of diverse sizes. In my view, when such common activities are institutionalized, they serve as arenas for democratic decision-making in a formal sense, and no langer remain merely casual or ad hoc. Democracy is thus a form of decision-making involving equal rights of participation among the members of a given community or institution. Gould "The Human Right to Democracy and its Global Impact," 292.

In the second criterion, Gould adapts the disputed all-affected principle that takes intensity and extensiveness in being affected by a collective problem or a policy question into concern. Gould *Globalizing Democracy and Human Rights*, 170. See further Gould, *Globalizing Democracy*, 171 ff, 35 ff; Gould, "Global Impact," 286, 292; Carol C. Gould, *Rethinking Democracy. Freedom and Social Cooperation in Politics, Economy, and Society* (Cambridge: Cambridge University Press, 1990).

[89] Gould, *Globalizing Democracy*, 178.

To overcome this circularity, "if we claim that the human rights to be considered as affected by a given decision or policy include democracy among others,"[90] she proposes to distinguish between two senses of democratic human rights: Democracy 1 (pertaining to the *common activity criterion* and standing for the requirement of equal participation in common decisions) and Democracy 2 (pertaining to the *relevantly affected criterion*, representing a "democratic input criterion" with a global coverage of distant others that must be included into decision-making if relevantly affected by a decision even if they are outside the democratic body that renders this very decision). According to Gould, circularity would be avoided, "since the claim would then be that Democracy 2 is required for the fulfillment of Democracy 1."[91] Finally, Gould provides us with an overview of the possible applications of her approach in transnational decision-making, namely democratization.[92] Gould's comprehensive, social conception of democracy and human rights allows us to bridge several gaps between agency-, capability-, and interest-based conceptions of human rights. Her wide focus on incorporating individual, societal, domestic, and global political levels into her considerations gives us an insight into the complex network aspects falling under the idea of global-reach democracy. However, it stays often obscure whether and to what degree the ideal kind of social relational ethos and the normative claims Gould imagines particularly depend on a *democratic* organization of the society. Gould's concrete democratization proposal—although it seems consistent—is highly prescriptive. If global democracy is feasible at all, the concrete implemen-

---

90 Gould, "Global Impact," 296–297.
91 Gould, "Global Impact," 296–297.
92 Gould proposes a fourfold global governance strategy. First, democratic procedures would need to be introduced into all (self-understood) communities and institutions, which are increasingly cross-border or transnational, whether global or not. Goals are a democratic culture and individuals democratic personalities, as an important principle serves the notion of subsidiarity, "with decisions to be taken at the most local levels possible, but where the local does not necessarily have a geographical interpretation, but instead one of proximity and size (recognizing that many of the new communities will cross borders)." Second, she proposes a global democratic parliament with the authority to implement a set of global shared ends. Third, she sees a need to devise new forms of public input and new modes of transnational representation within the institutions of global governance. In this context, she mentions the encouragement by NGOs as well as the use of deliberative software and other forms of online interaction or representative deliberative polling. Fourth, and in longer term, "the development of a system of delegate assemblies, based on the principles of subsidiarity, with real power to determine global policies, for example, concerning regulatory matters and labor politics" should be realized. For example, such assemblies could be "geographically based for some issues or could be functionally oriented, and would need to involve the election of delegates at higher levels." Gould, "Global Impact," 298–299.

tation of a legitimate project of global democracy would have to consist in a long-term transitional process justified step by step, over all a process that is democratically accepted and effectively demanded by people and peoples.

3.2 Instrumental moral conceptions

3.2.1 Empirical foundation of the moral claim for worldwide minimally egalitarian democracy (Thomas Christiano)

Thomas Christiano provides particularly important contributions to the HRD debate. His advocacy of the HRD is built on a composition of normative claims and empirical arguments. He draws on instrumental moral and political arguments. It is his insistence on the moral foundation of his HRD claim that supported the decision to put his approach into the category of instrumental moral (not political) conceptions. I will mainly refer to his two specific articles "An Instrumental Argument for a Human Right to Democracy"[93] and "An Egalitarian Argument for a Human Right to Democracy."[94] Christiano addresses two main objections against the HRD: (i) that the moral philosophical right to democracy conflicts with the law of the peoples to collective self-determination, and (ii) that new democracies often violate basic moral citizenship rights and are in danger to end up in tyranny of the majority (what comes down to a conflict between the HRD and other human rights). He refutes the first objection by claiming that democracies in general officiate as reliable protectors of urgent and broadly accepted basic human rights, and that non-democracies and partial democracies inevitably fail to protect these rights. Christiano's core assumption is that the moral HRD is based on, and legitimized by, its crucial role in protecting other fundamental moral rights in political and international societies. He goes on to give a threefold instrumental argument for democracy as a *moral* human right: i) the domestic peace argument, ii) the international significance argument, and iii) arguments against potential objections to potential objections to his instrumental arguments.[95]

---

[93] Thomas Christiano, "An Instrumental Argument for a Human Right to Democracy," 39(2) Philosophy and Public Affairs (2011), 142–176.
[94] Thomas Christiano, "An Egalitarian Argument for a Human Right to Democracy," in Cindy Holder and David Reidy (eds.) Human Rights: The Hard Questions (Cambridge: Cambridge University Press, 2013), 301–325.
[95] Christiano, "Instrumental Argument," 142–144.

According to Christiano, *rights of personal integrity* are presupposed; they comprise "an intuitive and widely accepted list of very urgent moral goods (the protections of the right not to be tortured, the right not to be arbitrarily imprisoned, and the rights not to be murdered or disappeared by the state)."[96] He argues that there is an HRD *because* "the institutional structure made up by the legal and conventional rights that constitute democracy are normally necessary and reliable in protecting basic rights to personal integrity and that thus it is strongly morally justified."[97] Christiano perceives a "strong moral justification for states to adopt or maintain the institutions of minimally egalitarian democracy and that it is morally justified for the international community to respect, protect, and promote the right of each person to participate in minimally egalitarian democratic decision making concerning their society."[98] A minimally egalitarian democracy is defined as a democracy with a (formal or informal) constitutional structure that ensures that individuals are able to participate as equals in the collective decision-making of their political society.[99] This conception of democracy includes a cluster of rights such as formally equal votes; equal opportunity to run for office, to determine the agenda of decision-making, and to influence the process of deliberation; and the freedom to organize, join, or abandon previous political associations. It further requires that there be robust competition among parties and a variety of represented parties in the legislature. The political actors (alike all public and private actors in society) must act in accordance with the rule of law. There must be an independent judiciary that checks on executive power. This cluster of rights, required for "minimally egalitarian democracy" is at the center of Christiano's claim for democracy.[100]

Taking a closer look at the threefold empirical and instrumental domestic peace argument, Christiano first explains that minimally egalitarian democracy is normally a reliable method of protecting the least controversial of human rights (personal integrity rights) and that societies whose institutions are not minimally egalitarian are normally unreliable in this respect. In contrast to other societies, minimally egalitarian democracies stand in a positive correlation with the protection of personal integrity rights and serve as an important independent variable explaining the protection of those rights. Furthermore, Christi-

---

[96] Christiano, "An Egalitarian Argument," 317.
[97] Christiano, "Instrumental Argument," 145.
[98] Christiano, "Instrumental Argument," 145–146.
[99] According to Christiano, a paradigm instance of minimally egalitarian democracy can be more precisely characterized by the following three conditions: Christiano, "Egalitarian Argument," 303.
[100] Christiano, "Egalitarian Argument," 303.

ano finds evidence to support the idea that one must first introduce minimally egalitarian democracy before the protection of human rights can become substantial, and he creates a model to show why minimally egalitarian democracy has these effects while other conceptions of democracy do not.[101]

Second, Christiano says that the international community has good moral reasons to be concerned with whether a society is democratic or not. He concludes that the international community is morally justified in protecting and promoting human rights of personal integrity; however, the international community must also find a moral justification for protecting and promoting minimally egalitarian democracy.[102] At this crucial stage in his argument, Christiano "asserts that democracies do not go to war with one another and that this distinguishes democracies from other types of regimes."[103] He thereby supports the idea that the widespread presence of democracy is a global collective good. Additionally, Christiano stresses the evidence that democratic regimes comply with international law and that they are more likely to create and sustain international institutions than non-democracies.[104]

Third, Christiano argues that the right to democracy should not be rejected, because it does not have any highly problematic effects on other rights.[105] With regard to the assessment of assumed general empirical advantages of democratic regimes, other scholars disagree significantly with Christiano. Beitz for example insists that the rights and peace guaranteeing quality of democratic regimes depends from the particular situational and historical circumstances in a country. He concludes that democratic structures alone are not reliable for a successful, politically stable transition. He's objection states that in many impoverished states, the process of democratization has stalled over the last thirty years and instead produced political regimes that are "as likely to violate the human rights to personal integrity as autocratic regimes."[106] The positive correlation between income and democracy is discussed by Beitz as one reason why the international community is not able to implement long-lasting democratization in poor countries. Replying to this objection, Christiano points out a number of successful transitions to democracy, and the constructive role the international community played in assisting in those transitions. Other research would show that poverty

---

[101] Christiano, "Instrumental Argument," 160.
[102] Christiano, "Instrumental Argument," 161.
[103] Christiano, "Instrumental Argument," 163.
[104] Christiano, "Instrumental Argument," 164.
[105] Christiano, "Instrumental Argument," 147–148.
[106] Christiano, "Instrumental Argument," 167.

does not seem to rule out a transition to effective democracy or the positive involvement of the international community.[107]

> Moreover, these arguments support the idea that democracies tend to protect the human rights to personal integrity even when per capita GDP is controlled for and the GDP is controlled for and that GDP per capita has a small effect on human rights protection.[108]

The challenges of the democratization of poor countries do not, according to Christiano, undermine the moral justification of the international community's attempts to carry it out. At the same time, however, a valid moral justification for democratizing intervention does not automatically translate into direct measures to carry it out.[109]

A second objection Christiano is confronted with says that democracy—even if it does better in some respects—does worse in others. Admitting that there might be some outlier cases, Christiano rejects them as irrelevant to the validity of the HRD: "So while the human right to democracy may be defeasible in highly unusual circumstances of large-scale failure, it normally serves as a constraint on the activities of officials."[110] The main objection is directed at a violation of legitimate self-determination that is caused by the moral commitment of the international community to protect and promote minimally egalitarian democracies, which, according to Cohen and others, amounts to intolerance toward non-democracies.[111] By defining legitimate collective self-determination as a type of self-determination that implicitly assumes the society's respect for human rights, and by stating that legitimate self-determination further implies that conditions of unanimity and broad participation are (from a realist standpoint) a sufficient, but not necessary, condition, Christiano finds no evidence for the HRD limiting the legitimate right to collective self-determination:[112]

> In reply to the objection, the first thing to note is that ... there is substantial reason to think that, in tolerating nondemocratic societies, citizens of democratic societies are tolerating

---

107 Christiano, "Instrumental Argument," 167–168.
108 Christiano, "Instrumental Argument," 168.
109 Christiano forms an analogy between parents and the international community to illustrate his point:
To have a moral justification for attempting to achieve a certain outcome X does not entail that one must always be doing something to achieve X. Parents have a moral justification to try to get their children to be decent human beings. But there are many times when it is best to stand back and hope for the best." Christiano, "Instrumental Argument," 169.
110 Christiano, "Instrumental Argument," 171.
111 Christiano, "Instrumental Argument," 172.
112 Christiano, "Instrumental Argument," 172.

societies that normally violate uncontroversial and very urgent human rights. In the normal case, the toleration of nondemocracies amounts to the toleration of severe human rights violations or of the high probability that such violations will occur. Normally, the absence of minimally egalitarian democracy seems to imply the absence of legitimate collective self-determination.[113]

While Christiano outright claims that nonessential assistance to non-democratic states can only be offered only on the condition that they take steps toward democratization, he insists that cooperation can start in a variety of ways and that minimally egalitarian democracy does not necessarily mean perfect democracy or perfect justice. Minimally egalitarian democracy would also be compatible, for example, with consociational and majoritarian democracies; presidential and parliamentary systems; proportional representation; and single-member district representation. In all legitimate forms of minimally egalitarian democracy, the fundamental rights of persons serve as substantial limits.[114]

In his subsequent article Christiano expands his claim by showing that the traditional argument for democracy holds even for those societies that do not accept the principle of equality.[115] Distinguishing between democracy at the domestic level and democracy at the international level, he reaffirms the two "sufficient" conditions for the human right to democracy: first, that every society ought to realize democratic rights and, second, that the international community is morally justified in trying to realize democracy in every society, "because only in this way can the international community itself make law for its members that is democratically legitimate and only in this way can democratic societies make law for themselves that is fully democratically legitimate."[116] However, he then mitigates the requirement of collective self-determination and toleration for the non-democratic societies. The weaker conception of collective self-determination still allows the instrumental argument of freedom from forced, or other forms of, intervention; the notion of toleration is understood as non-intervention in non-democratic countries (although it implies unreserved cooperation of societies with a full equality in the international realm).[117] A further mitigation concerns the insight that it is important for a society to develop democratic institu-

---

113 Christiano, "Instrumental Argument," 173.
114 Christiano, "Instrumental Argument," 174.
115 Christiano, "Egalitarian Argument," 301.
116 Christiano, "Egalitarian Argument," 317.
117 Christiano, "Egalitarian Argument," 323.

tions on its own because homegrown democratic institutions are more stable and satisfying than externally imposed ones.[118]

At this point, it is important to come back to Amartya Sen's oft quoted empirical, instrumental argument that democracies have a significant effect on prevention of economic and social disasters such as famine. Sen highlighted the significant correlation between political and civil rights and the prevention of major economic disasters by showing that political and civil rights give people the opportunity to compel governments to attend to general needs and engage in appropriate public action:

> The response of a government to the acute suffering of its people often depends on the pressure that is put on it. The exercise of political rights (such as voting, criticizing, protesting, and the like) can make a real difference to the political incentives that operate on a government.[119]

Rejecting the "Lee hypothesis," which says that non-democratic systems are better at bringing about economic development, Sen points out that the political incentives provided by democratic governance acquire great practical value especially in periods of crisis. In general, democracy enhances the capacity of people's demand of political action (including the satisfaction of their economic needs) to be heard.[120] As shown earlier, Sen's human rights conception exceeds the instrumental argumentation. However, according to Allan Buchanan, Amartya Sen's work provides the best support for the argument that democratic governance is the most reliable instrument of ensuring that human rights are respected.[121]

Christiano's egalitarian conception, however, which tries to prove that equal consideration of interests depends on minimal democracy, has been criticized for insufficiently elaborating the deduction of collective, group-rights-based self-determination from the principle of individual equality.[122] The lack of a clear distinction between empirical findings at an international level and conclusions based on normative principles make the argument unclear. Subsequent to Beitz's criticism, given the uneven findings and several cases of failed democra-

---

118 Christiano, "Egalitarian Argument," 323.
119 Sen, "Democracy as a Universal Value," 7.
120 Sen, "Democracy as a Universal Value," 7–10.
121 Allan Buchanan, *Justice, Legitimacy, and Self-determination* (Oxford: Oxford University Press, 2007), 143.
122 Andrew Altman and Christopher Heath Wellman, *A Liberal Theory of International Justice* (Oxford: Oxford University Press, 2009), 21–22.

tization in poor countries, empirical advantages of well-functioning democracies do not sufficiently support a claim of a (moral) HRD. Unfortunately, little attention has been paid to cultural and historical differences between democratic and non-democratic cultures and values, or to the question of how the mediation between both could be realized. The latter is important as it provides the basis for legitimate universal human rights claimed on the basis of one's own *democratic* convictions.

3.2.2 Individual moral autonomy needs "rule by the people" (Robert Dahl)

Whereas Christiano combines empirical and theoretical claims, Robert Dahl starts with an explicit distinction between theoretical- and political-reality-oriented considerations. It is particularly difficult to place his approach on the fourfold conceptual map, because it straddles the instrumental and the intrinsic moral standpoints. In fact, Dahl's use of intrinsic moral arguments would justify putting his proposal in either category: moral intrinsic and moral instrumental. Dahl's argumentation aims to separate the evaluative comparison of democratic and hierarchical governmental systems (the reality-dimension) from the theoretical comparison of ideal democracy and ideal paternalism. Dahl wants to prove the hypothesis that democratic systems can be justified by the fact that they make it possible to optimally approximate an ideal political system with the view to safeguarding the interests of citizens.

> A hardheaded look at human experience, historical and contemporary, shows that among political societies that have actually existed, or now exist, those that most nearly satisfy the criteria of the democratic idea are, taken all around, better than the rest.[123]

Dahl starts from the basic assumption that social cohabitation takes a common decision-making procedure for granted, which allows us to determine principles, rules, laws, and political solutions that are collectively binding for all members. He draws a comparison between *guardianship* and *democracy* as two contrasting models for structuring political processes. The paternalistic variant of government, guardianship, means that a small elite with special capabilities, knowledge, and virtues is authorized to rule. The democratic variant is defined as the "rule by the people" (by the demos). Citizens are thereby considered equals for the purposes of arriving at governmental decisions.[124] Dahl takes the *intrinsic*

---

[123] Robert A. Dahl, *Democracy and Its Critics* (New Haven: Yale University Press, 1989), 84.
[124] Dahl, *Democracy and Its Critics*, 83.

equality, understood as the principle of equal consideration of human interests, as his criterion for evaluating political systems.[125] The three fundamental human interests are: the achievement of maximum feasible freedom, the possibility to fully develop one's capacities and potentialities as a human being, and the satisfaction of other interests within the limits of feasibility and fairness to others. Dahl key claim is that democracy constitutes an essential means of satisfying these fundamental interests, even though not a sufficient condition for achieving them.[126] He then goes on to distinguish three instrumental functions of democracy: providing maximum feasible freedom, fostering human development, and protecting personal interests.

A strong historical correlation between democracy and freedom leads Dahl to derive the first of three functions of democracy: ensuring the maximum of freedom. The logic of a democratic system inherently comprises a fairly broad range of important rights such as rights to free expression, political organization, opposition, and fair and free elections. These formal presuppositions do not exist in isolation but require a political culture that supports the democratic order.[127]

> As a result of the rights inherently required for the democratic process, together with a political culture and a broader domain of personal freedom associated with that process, democracy tends to provide a more extensive domain of personal freedom than any other kind of regime can promise.[128]

Apart from a general (political) freedom, democracy serves to enhance the freedom of self-determination and moral autonomy. Self-determination (i.e. self-governance, capacity for obeying laws one has set oneself) and moral autonomy are both considered to be desirable ends.[129] A morally autonomous person is understood to be one who is self-governing in the domain of morally relevant choices, "who decides on his moral principles, and the decisions that significantly depend on them, following a process of reflection, deliberation, scrutiny, and consideration."[130]

The beneficial effect of democracy on the development of desirable qualities in citizens (the second function of democracy) is derived from John Stuart Mill's

---

[125] Dahl, *Democracy and Its Critics*, 86–87.
[126] Dahl, *Democracy and Its Critics*, 88.
[127] Dahl, *Democracy and Its Critics*, 88–89.
[128] Dahl, *Democracy and Its Critics*, 89.
[129] Dahl, *Democracy and Its Critics*, 89–91.
[130] Dahl, *Democracy and Its Critics*, 91.

vision that it should be a priority of a good government to promote the virtue and intelligence of its subjects. Dahl himself admits that this effect relies on a mere empirical hypothesis that remains to be confirmed.[131]

In his discussion of the capacity of democracies to protect personal interests (the third function), Dahl argues that democratic governments tend to satisfy a minimal set of urgent political concerns of citizens. By providing "an orderly and peaceful process by means of which a majority of citizens can influence the government to do what they most want it to do and to avoid doing what they most want it not to do" [132], democratic governments also commit themselves to respond to the urgent concerns of their citizens. Neglecting these urgent political needs and underlying personal interests would foster protest and dissatisfaction with the democratic representatives.

The argument saying that democracy is the best governmental system to protect and promote personal autonomy in the political process depends on the assumption that the (ordinary) people in general are equally qualified to govern themselves.[133] Following a "rule of prudence," Dahl states the presumption of personal autonomy, which says that every adult must be treated as if he were the best possible judge if a decision concerning his own interests: "In the absence of a compelling showing to the contrary everyone should be assumed to be the best judge of his or her own good or interest."[134]

Dahl's reasoning provides a textbook example of a liberal democratic justification of democracy. While the theoretical side of his model allows to argue in universal terms, the practical side of the model falls short. In addition to several objections Dahl himself raises, the broadest criticism must be directed at the strong liberal democratic ideals that Dahl claims are unassailable. Building a democratic government in a country that does not follow the enlightenment tradition would ignore the historical experience of democratization as well as the "self-evident" insight that moral autonomy is necessarily a supreme value for human beings. Dahl's approach is nevertheless helpful in unpacking the classical value assumptions which more or less explicitly undergird most HRD claims. The guarantee of personal autonomy is paradigmatically proved to necessarily depend on the presupposition of a democratically structured political system.

Apart from the subject-oriented moral argument that seems to support an HRD, it is important to highlight that Dahl himself denies the possibility of a functioning *global* democracy: "Can international organizations, institutions,

---

[131] Dahl, *Democracy and Its Critics*, 92.
[132] Dahl, *Democracy and Its Critics*, 95.
[133] Dahl, *Democracy and Its Critics*, 97.
[134] Dahl, *Democracy and Its Critics*, 100.

or processes be democratic? – I argue that they cannot be."[135] One of his arguments is that the size of democratic units correlates with the influence of citizens' participation,[136] and that international foreign politics issues are often to abstract and complex to be truly integrated in democratic political culture.[137] Popular control of foreign affairs is almost impossible to realize. Another important reason for the rejection of international democracy lies in the mutual interdependence between substantial and procedural solutions in a functioning democracy.[138] According to Dahl, a functioning democracy depends on the presumption of a public good; the right (procedural solutions) and the good (substantive solutions) condition each other. To claim the possibility of consensus about public good in foreign affairs is overreaching. Therefore, Dahl proposes that international institutions primarily gain their legitimation not through democratic organization but through a model of well-reflected guardianship:

> If we judge that important human needs require an international organization, despite its costs to democracy, we should not only subject its undemocratic aspects to scrutiny and criticism but also try to create proposals for greater democratization and insist that they be adopted.[139]

Dahl argues that the merits of international organizations should not rely on a democratic structure, as long as they contribute to public human good. This insight entails the idea that legitimate democratization depends on its internal support of political culture. Therefore, for the current world situation, Dahl proposes a trade-off between ongoing educative assistance in democratization and a re-evaluative, well-thought-out *modus operandi* of (non-democratic) institutions.

---

135 Robert Dahl, "Can International Organizations Be Democratic?," in Ian Shapiro and Casiano Hacker-Cordon (eds), *Democracy's Edges* (Cambridge: Cambridge University Press, 1999), 19.
136 Dahl, "Can International Organizations Be Democratic?," 22:
    In both democratic theory and practice a fundamental dilemma lurks half hidden, ordinarily just out of view. Other things being more or less equal, a smaller democratic unit provides an ordinary citizen with greater opportunities to participate in governing than a larger unit. But the smaller the unit the more likely that some matters of importance to the citizen are beyond the capacity of the government to deal with effectively. To handle these broader matters, the democratic unit might be enlarged; but in doing so the capacity of the citizen to participate effectively in governing would be diminished. To put it loosely, one might say that although your government gains more control over the problem, your capacity to influence that government is diminished.
137 Dahl, "Can International Organizations Be Democratic?," 23–24.
138 Dahl, "Can International Organizations Be Democratic?," 25–26.
139 Dahl, "Can International Organizations Be Democratic?," 34.

3.2.3 International demoi-cracy on the grounds of a legal human right to democracy (Samantha Besson)

In contrast to Dahl's skepticism about international institutional democracy, Samantha Besson provides an account that is based on a necessity of international-*demoicracy*. In giving an ambitiously synthesis of the HRD debate, Besson postulates a moral HRD that must be transposed into an international legal HRD.[140] She points out that the moral and political views could and should become mediated by a legal perspective. Her initial stipulation is, that—given the already existing democratic human rights (Article III of the Declaration of the Rights of Man and of the Citizen, Article 21 of the Universal Declaration of Human Rights, Article 25 of the International Covenant on Civil and Political Rights)—the question whether there *is* a legal Human Right to Democracy in international law has become superfluous. A potent question that remains to be answered is whether there *should* be at all an international or universal human right to political participation.[141] Besson proposes an "interest-based theory ... modified by reference to considerations of moral-political status in a given community":[142]

> More specifically, the proposed account is moral in the independent justification it provides for human rights and political in the function it sees them vested with as both shields against the state and guarantees of political inclusion. In terms of justification, its moral-political dimension differs both from accounts based on a purely ethical justification of human rights, and from accounts that seek a political form of minimalist justification of human rights.[143]

The account that is neither fish ("moral") nor fowl ("political") is promised to salvage the political role of human rights without diluting their moral justification. However, this account is said to provide "useful insights about legal human rights."[144] Besson defines legal rights as legally protected moral interests, and understands "the human right to democracy" as shorthand for a human right

---

[140] Samantha Besson, "The Human Right to Democracy – A Moral Defence with a Legal Nuance," Paper presented at Conference "Definition and Development of Human Rights and Popular Sovereignty in Europe (Frankfurt a.M., 2013), 6.
[141] Besson orients her approach explicitly at an international or universal human right to democratic participation but not ("as it has been traditionally the case") to a national or local right to democratic participation. Besson, "The Human Right to Democracy," 3, 6.
[142] Besson, "The Human Right to Democracy," 9.
[143] Besson, "The Human Right to Democracy," 9.
[144] Besson, "The Human Right to Democracy," 9.

to a given democratic interest. She argues for a moral right to democracy *qua* international human right to democratic participation. She then goes on to give several reasons for the legal recognition of a moral right to democracy, including security, clarity, and intermediary agreement on a contested right or set of interests, effectivity, sanctions, and publicity.

According to Besson, the legalization of the right to democracy would enhance its realization in practice: it would enable democratic processes through legal directives and at same time protect such directives "against themselves and their own making."[145] The legal recognition of the moral right to democracy should then take place through international, rather than national, law. Besson gives four primary reasons for the international legalization:

> (i) its personal scope as international human rights have individuals as right-holders, but also other states and international organizations in the international community (through *erga omnes* duties of the state or through conventional duties based on a human rights treaty), first, and have all individuals residing in a given state and not only citizens as right-holders, second; (ii) its material scope as international human rights law may fill gaps in national protection or at least provide a minimal safety net in case of human rights relapse in a given state; and (iii) its territorial scope as international human rights law protect not only individuals within state boundaries, but also all individuals submitted to its extra-territorial jurisdiction. (iv) Additional reasons may also be found in the international mechanisms available to enforce international human rights duties, whether political or judicial and whether coercive or non-coercive and military or non-military. As Buchanan and Russell have interestingly captured, further reasons may be identified and grouped into self-regarding reasons and other-regarding or cosmopolitan reasons.[146]

The practical advantages of an institutionalized commitment to the HRD claim presuppose democracy to be a common interest of states and individuals. The democratic legitimation process of an international human right to democracy is seen as advancing in a process of itineration and development. What seems to be a prima facie circular (setting an international human right to democracy as a universal interest of all states without de facto democratic recognition) is only of temporary appearance in Bessons view. She sees the relationship between international demoi-cracy and the international legal right to democracy as one of mutual reinforcement rather than one of logical sequence, as a virtuous circle:

> Of course, the more democratic, or rather the more *demoi*-cratic international human rights law-making and human rights law enforcement becomes, the more legitimate the interna-

---

145 Besson, "The Human Right to Democracy," 21.
146 Besson, "Moral Defence," 22.

tional legal right to democracy will be. In a global community of states and individuals, growing interdependencies imply mutually affected interests and hence generate the interest and claim of states and individuals to decide together over those issues and no longer on their own and separately or only very indirectly together. In those circumstances, inclusion and participation at all levels, including the national one, becomes a legitimate individual claim and, at the same time, participation in the decision-making process stems as a common interest. If those conditions pertain, the right to democratic participation will no longer be an interest over which only national democratic polities can decide, but an interest of the community of communities.[147]

By referencing the virtuous, mutually reinforcing relation between international *demoi-cracy* and the international legal right to democracy, Besson addresses the complexity of the factual international political situation and decides in favor of a commitment to an original, authoritative positing in international law. In a more systematic way than Christiano (who frequently oscillates between empirical and moral philosophical arguments), she argues on the level of the moral, the political, but additionally on the legal dimension in favor of the claim to a HRD. Both authors account for the constitutive and entangled logics of individual and collective self-determination. Christiano shows the reciprocal interdependency through his conceptualization of minimally egalitarian democracy. Minimally egalitarian democracy serves as a minimal condition of human rights and personal integrity protection. Additionally, it structures the players' cooperation within the international political system. Besson hones the argument by pointing out the mutual reinforcement mechanism between international *demoi-cracy* and the international legal right to democracy. As soon as one assumes that the international community campaigns for a cooperative multilateral system that accounts for democratic principles (international *demoi-cracy*), the claim for an international legal right to democracy must necessarily follow. However, compared to Dahl, Besson's approach falls short of realist consideration of human limits of cognition, learning, and motivation. Her steadfast belief in a self-referential logic of democracy (which is supposed to work by courtesy of presumed individuals compliance as soon as it has been procedurally institutionalized and guaranteed) pays little attention to cultural differences, non-Western patterns and community structures, and international feasibility of democratization in general. In my view, Besson rightly insists on separating the moral, political, and legal dimensions of human rights. However, she fails to draw a most original and important conclusion, namely, that a moral set of human rights should be defined as a set of values (point of ideal orientation) that is in-

---

147 Besson, "Moral Defence," 22.

tentionally understood to be more comprehensive than the set of institutionalized legal and political human rights, and that it therefore must not necessarily be thought of as congruent with a set of legal or political human rights.

3.2.4 The right to democracy is no fundamental human right (Richard J. Arneson)

Richard J. Arneson challenges the classical liberal-democratic, moral-instrumental views that endorse the HRD claim; he is, as he puts it, "swimming upstream" by arguing against the "pretheoretical common sense position," which states "that democracy as a political decision procedure is morally justified partly because this procedure is inherently fair and partly because its operation leads to desirable consequences."[148] His response specifically targets Christopher P. Griffin's argument in a debate of the *Journal of Political Philosophy*. Griffin claims that democracy is intrinsically merely a political procedure because its rules and practices treat persons in accordance with the requirements of justice:[149]

> The argument sketched here for viewing democracy as a requirement of justice involves translating equal basic moral status into equal shares of political power—one person, one vote in a majoritarian decision rule. I claim that equality in the distributive shares of political power represents an appropriate extension of equality of basic moral status to equality of basic social standing.[150]

Arneson rejects the claim of intrinsic fairness of democratic procedures, insisting that there is nothing intrinsically fair about the procedure of one person–one vote that would have to be traded against the goal of producing better consequences.[151] Arneson is skeptical that only democracy of choice could express the idea that persons have equal basic moral status, and he views the moral assessment of a choice as dependent on whether this choice is supported by good moral reasons. Procedural democratic conditions alone are not sufficient to produce just outcomes. Like all other procedures, democratic procedures should be evaluated "according to the moral value of the outcomes they would be reason-

---

[148] Richard J. Arneson, "Debate: Defending the Purely Instrumental Account of Democratic Legitimacy," 11(1) Journal of Political Philosophy (2003): 130.
[149] Christopher P. Griffin, "Democracy as a Non-Instrumentally Just Procedure," 11(1) Journal of Political Philosophy (2003): 118.
[150] Griffin, "Democracy as a Non-Instrumentally Just Procedure," 118.
[151] Arneson, "Debate," 130.

ably expected to produce."[152] The promotion of individual rights serves as a criterion for selecting specific governmental institutions. The message expressed by a practice "depends on what is reasonable to suppose that those to whom the message is communicated will take its meaning to be."[153] Arneson calls his favored instrumental approach to the justification of democracy the "best-results account of political legitimacy."[154] Because the exercise of the vote is considered to be an exercise of power, and because fundamental moral rights do not include rights of power over others, Arneson stipulates that the moral right to democracy should not be included among fundamental moral rights.[155] He suggests that excluding the right to having a say in a democracy amounts to constraining the already narrow content of fundamental moral rights.[156] Arneson gives clear priority to the fundamental moral rights the content of which has to be determined at a more abstract and general level than procedures and institutions.[157] His distinction between fundamental moral rights and non-fundamental political, legal rights to guarantee these moral rights, allows him to advocate the strong statement that fundamental moral rights are intrinsically valuable and worthy of being recognized independently of whether are acknowledged by means of a (specific) political procedure or by means of their manifestation as legal rights. Such a conceptual distinction proves consistency in argumentation. However, discussing the strong historical connection between the moral individual rights and the development of democratic institutions is important, along with the discussion about to whom moral authority is assigned (and to what extent), and how it becomes enforced.

---

152 Richard J. Arneson, "Democratic Rights at the National and Workplace Levels," in David Copp, Jean Hampton, and John E. Roemer (eds), *The Idea of Democracy*, (Cambridge: Cambridge University Press, 1995), 118–148, 125, cited by Griffin.
153 Arneson, "Debate," 132.
154 Arneson, "Debate," 123.
155 Arneson, "Debate," 124–125.
156 See Arneson, "Debate," 125:
  This stipulation is supposed to accomplish two things. First, I rule out the rights to a democratic say (an equal vote in a democratic political procedure) as a candidate for the status of fundamental moral right. Second, I intend that the exclusion of the right to a democratic say is not arbitrary but part of a principled and reasonable minimal constraint on the content of fundamental moral rights. Whatever rights we deem fundamental, important to satisfy just for their own sake "rights" or purported rights to exercise power over other people's lives should not be included within the set of fundamental rights.
157 Arneson, "Debate," 129.

3.2.5. A minimalist human rights claim to democracy: a human right to (some kind of) political participation (David Miller)

David Miller contributes to the HRD debate with his *National Responsibility and Global Justice*,[158] published in 2007, and his recent working paper[159] which directly addresses the question. Miller accepts the right to political participation as a justified moral human right, whereas he sees the right to democratic citizenship as a right only specific to liberal societies.[160] Against the backdrop of basic human needs, Miller directly opposes the option of an "authoritative" positing of a human right to democracy, for example in the body of international law.[161] According to the human needs approach, something is proved to be a human right if the enjoyment of that right fulfils the basic needs of the right-holder.[162] Human rights are instrumental in guaranteeing the satisfaction of basic human needs. Miller's "humanitarian strategy" takes basic human needs as a common foundation of human rights; among these human needs, physical and biological needs are the easiest to identify. In addition, Miller claims that an adequate list of human rights must include the idea of a minimally decent human life that has not just physical but also social components. The basic human needs must be recognized as "morally compelling by people everywhere whatever their own particular religious or secular world view."[163] The humanitarian strategy "identifies and justifies human rights by fixing on universal features of human beings that can serve as a ground for these rights."[164] Miller proceeds from a descriptive premise to a normative conclusion. According to him, a non-deductive argument can nonetheless be a valid moral argument:

---

[158] David Miller, *National Responsibility and Global Justice* (Oxford: Oxford University Press, 2007).
[159] David Miller, "Is there a Human Right to Democracy?," Centre for the Study of Social Justice (CSSJ) Working Paper Series, SJ032 (2015), 1–22.
[160] Miller, *National Responsibility and Global Justice*, 196–197.
[161] Miller, *National Responsibility and Global Justice*, 167 ff.
[162] Miller, *National Responsibility and Global Justice*, 179:
  But what does it mean to have a need? To play such a justificatory role, the needs in question must be what I have elsewhere called 'intrinsic' needs, as opposed to merely instrumental needs which get their moral force from the contingent ends that they serve. A person's intrinsic needs are those items or conditions it is necessary for a person to have if she is to avoid being harmed—thus food is an intrinsic need because in its absence people suffer the harms of hunger and malnutrition.
[163] Miller, *National Responsibility and Global Justice*, 169.
[164] Miller, *National Responsibility and Global Justice*, 179.

"People suffer extreme pain when they are tortured; therefore they have a right not to be tortured" is a valid moral argument, even though it is logically possible to assert the premise and deny the conclusion. I shall take it for granted that such arguments that ground rights in empirical features of human beings are at least potentially valid.[165]

Irrespective of the question whether such a by-the-way neglect of the Humean is–ought distinction can be dropped without further explanation, the need for empirical evidence to justify basic human needs limits the coverage of human rights substantially. Democratic rights, such as the right to equal participation, seem insufficient to guarantee the basic human rights needed for a minimally decent human life.[166] Despite having identified the human right to participation as a legitimate human rights claim, Miller puts it in an inferior category of social needs, whereby civil rights, rather then human rights, are justified:

> In drawing this line between basic human rights and the longer list that can be found in some human rights documents, I am assuming that only certain rights-violations are urgent enough to trigger remedial responsibilities in outsiders: being denied material subsistence triggers such responsibilities, whereas being denied equal participation in politics does not.[167]

The needs-based justification of human rights cannot fully account for the value of civil and political rights but has to be justified via the construct of societal needs and corresponding citizenship rights. Miller promotes this distinction in order to remain faithful to his own obligation to provide a human rights conception covering "the global minimum," and thus plays a central role "in any theory of global justice."[168] However, Miller's aspiration to provide a conception of human rights that is general enough to achieve practical agreement across societies and cultures, and that therefore could be legitimately claimed as obligatory for states to respect, goes hand in hand with his skepticism toward the suggestion that international law should be seen as an authoritative source of obligatory human rights. He describes the content of international law to be a matter of interpretation forbidding to "obtain a definitive ruling on, for example, the question whether there is a human right to democracy."[169]

In contrast to his updated position, in *National Responsibility and Global Justice*, the absence of the human right to political participation is clearly declared

---

[165] Miller, *National Responsibility and Global Justice*, 180.
[166] Miller, *National Responsibility and Global Justice*, 180–181.
[167] Miller, *National Responsibility and Global Justice*, 168.
[168] Miller, *National Responsibility and Global Justice*, 197.
[169] Miller, *National Responsibility and Global Justice*, 171.

not to "harm" humans in fulfillment of intrinsic needs. Its justification as a human right is due to its instrumental function as secondary protection of more basic human conditions and needs.[170] Thus, Miller suggests a two-level account distinguishing between human rights and citizenship rights. The former cover the basic human needs, the latter cover the societal needs with which the social justice, civil, and political rights within political communities are associated. The right to participation seems still ambiguously classified. On the one hand, the right to participation falls into the category of political and civil rights that respond to societal needs; on the other, it is identified as a legitimate human rights claim because of its function as a secondary protection of other human rights.[171]

Proceeding from his earlier thoughts about the right to participation to the question whether there should be a human right to democracy, Miller opens his recent article by supporting the relevance of the HRD-debate. He starts off by conceptualizing the HRD as a claim for democratic institutions rather then as a mere claim for membership and participation. He then extracts the human right to participation as question that needs to be asked separately.[172] He points out that, from a moral philosophical standpoint, we need to clarify whether democracy matters to us "instrumentally," for other goods and values it helps to promote, or whether it matters "for its own sake."[173] Thus, evaluating whether the institutional arrangement of democracy is justified requires an exploration of the grounds of human rights. As a second reason, Miller appeals to a need for awareness for possible practical consequences of such a claim, namely the moral responsibility to ensure that the human right to democracy was realized:

> If there is indeed a human right to democracy, and if, as many believe, for a state to be politically legitimate it must respect human rights, it immediately follows that the many undemocratic states that exist in today's world are illegitimate, and don't deserve the respect that we owe to all legitimate states. This would undermine the position of those like John Rawls in *The Law of Peoples* who envisage a pluralistic but tolerant world in which liberal democracies co-exist on terms of mutual respect with "decent hierarchical societies" whose political institutions are not democratic.[174]

---

170 Miller, *National Responsibility and Global Justice*, 195.
171 Miller, *National Responsibility and Global Justice*, 196.
172 Miller, *National Responsibility and Global Justice*, 4, 11, 15.
173 Miller, *National Responsibility and Global Justice*, 2.
174 Miller, *National Responsibility and Global Justice*, 2.

As pointed out in the book's introduction, these well-justified concerns about the feasibility and legitimacy of a project of global democratization, arising from a human right to democratic institutions, represent a basic caveat within the debate, if one emphasizes the political philosophical dimension of the HRD-question. Miller proceeds from a concept of democracy understood as "systems that are today conventionally regarded as democracies."[175] Such systems are supposed to maintain three features: (1) a constitution that guarantees fundamental rights and specifies the powers of each institution; (2) the presence of a range of freedoms; and (3) a decision-making mechanism, either direct or through representatives, based on political equality and majority rule.[176] Discussing the moral justification of an HRD claim, these three elements of democracy had to be of essential instrumental or intrinsic value in fulfilling basic needs for the HRD to be a justified human rights candidate. Miller rejects the instrumental value of a human right to democracy for several empirical reasons. He mainly argues that a peremptory demand for democratic institutions runs the risk of declaring as illegitimate already existing (non-democratic) institutions that nevertheless currently provide the best available protection of human rights.[177] The assumption of an intrinsic value of democracy for human beings is discussed on the basis of Allan Buchanan's version of the principle of moral equality. According to this principle, every person as such is worthy of equal regard. Thus, the requirement arises for all persons to receive the same fundamental status, as equal participants, in the most important political decisions made in their societies.[178] Democracy, understood as a system guaranteeing political equality and the majority rule, is therefore seen as an important element of the institutional recognition of the equality of persons. In essence, Miller argues against assuming equal status as a universal principle. He identifies it with a particular self-understanding of Western liberal societies that has not taken hold elsewhere.[179] Adopting John Stuart Mill's argument about voting, he concludes that the only legitimate human rights claim for democracy is one that provides that nobody be excluded from political participation:

> [We] can argue that from a human rights perspective, what is essential is that no-one should be excluded from political participation. So there is a human right to political inclusion, which is more than just the right to free political expression. Since the right's purpose

---

175 Miller, *National Responsibility and Global Justice*, 6.
176 Miller, *National Responsibility and Global Justice*, 6.
177 Miller, *National Responsibility and Global Justice*, 10.
178 Miller, *National Responsibility and Global Justice*, 11.
179 Miller, *National Responsibility and Global Justice*, 14.

is to contribute to the overall effectiveness of the set of human rights, it must give the right-holder the power to check those who make political decisions, for example by removing them from office, or voting against the decisions they have made in a referendum. So the human right must include the right to vote in some form, but not necessarily in the form favoured in Western democracies, where it means specifically the right to choose political representatives through equal votes in geographical constituencies."[180]

Miller's current position approaches the Cohen's right to membership. Proposing a human right to participation that includes more then free political expression—namely also the right to be heard and represented in one's own interest—represents an even more convincing version of Cohen's human rights claim of political inclusion. As Miller explains, such a right "might be fulfilled in a system in which representation was tailored to protect the interests of specific religious, ethnic or national groups, for example, in a consociational arrangement which gave these groups control or veto rights in areas of policy of special concern to them."[181] As such, even if viewed as a group right, the right to participation seems also compatible with a minimal (individual) human rights claim to voice in the face of an experience of severe injustice (meted out by the injured individual's group or government).

3.2.6 The human right to democracy belongs to the group of basic human rights (William Talbott)

William Talbott argues in *Which Rights Should Be Universal?* that the human capacity for judgment serves as an (historical) experience-based reference point for deriving and guaranteeing human rights. Talbott provides a list of nine basic sets of rights, the last of which includes "political rights, including democratic rights and an independent judiciary to enforce the entire package of rights."[182] Such a straightforward promotion of democratic rights as human rights is rare to find even in "intrinsic moral philosophers." Upon closer look, Talbott's justification —not of human rights in general but of the HRD in particular—relies more on the instrumental than on the intrinsic argumentation. This makes him another author who works at the boundary between intrinsic and instrumental conceptions. Talbott favors an *equilibrium model of epistemic justification*[183] which

---

180 Miller, *National Responsibility and Global Justice*, 15.
181 Miller, *National Responsibility and Global Justice*, 15.
182 Miller, *National Responsibility and Global Justice*, 178.
183 William J. Talbott, *Which Rights Should be Universal?* (Oxford: Oxford University Press, 2005), 29–30.

bridges consequentialist and non-consequentialist rationales. He bases his approach on Rawls, Habermas, and Mill. His key premise behind the claim for democratic rights is that human beings have a *first-person authority*. Moral inquiry proceeds primarily by bottom-up reasoning elaborated in an ongoing historical-social process and characterized by raising awareness of human conditions and social, collective, and transnational interdependences.[184] The rights-respecting democracy is identified to be the adequate political system allowing first-person authority to be exercised and the awareness of social and collective considerations to grow. These originally Mill's ideas state that it is a "universally true empirical fact that over long haul and given favorable background conditions normally competent adult human beings know best when it comes to judgments regarding their own good and well-being."[185] Against this, Reidy objected that the Mill's claim of an individual's first-person epistemic authority is not necessarily bound to democratic restrictions of political authority:

> Now, even if we accept as true this Millian claim regarding each individual's first-person epistemic authority when it comes to judgments regarding her own good, it's not obvious that only democracies can reliably advance the common good of their members.[186]

Against that view, Talbott objected on the one hand that claiming first-person authority does not imply that one can be infallible in moral judgments. The justification of strongly universal moral principles is thus social and historically verified rather than individualistic, "for we depend on others for information about the various social practices that exist and have existed, and even more, we depend on others to imagine possibilities that, by ourselves, we never would have imagined."[187] The experience of democratic exchange between the citizens, however, is important to any individual and political judgments with an authoritative aspiration.

Talbott is arguing for universal human rights against the background of a "historical-social process of moral discovery paradigm."[188] He sees the guiding idea behind human rights in enabling all people's conduct to develop and exer-

---

[184] Talbott, *Which Rights Should be Universal?*, 186.
[185] David Reidy, "Philosophy and Human Rights: Contemporary Perspectives," in Claudio Corradetti (ed.), *Philosophical Dimensions of Human Rights. Some Contemporary Views* (Dordrecht: Springer, 2012), 39.
[186] David A. Reidy, "On the Human Right to Democracy: Searching for Sense Without Stilts," 43(2) Journal of Social Philosophy (2012), 177–203, 196.
[187] Talbott, *Which Rights Should be Universal*, 33.
[188] Talbott, *Which Rights Should be Universal*, 35.

cise autonomy, to become the authors of their own lives.[189] Despite his basic commitment to the value of autonomy, as Talbotts consideration about the ninth basic right of his lists shows, the claim for political, democratic rights (as compared to the other eight basic rights of the list) is not that stringent to derive from such a basic claim as it could be expected. Autonomy serves as a marginal, rather than a decisive, argument to claim democratic rights. Talbott develops three conventional arguments to legitimize democratic rights: *autonomy*, *procedure*, and *results*.[190] He himself argues for a package of political rights including democratic rights that are particularly *founded on the results oriented focus*, because of reservations against both the autonomy- and the procedure-oriented argument. The *autonomy* a person gains through her right to vote is often a very low-impact contribution proportional to the thousands of others inputs in the final decision.[191] The problem with a pro-HRD argumentation based on *procedural* advantages of democratic rights is that they alone cannot morally justify an outcome. Defending the importance of democratic rights in procedural terms means to hold that a procedure in which each affected person has an equal voice in determining the outcome legitimates the outcome.[192] Talbott illustrates the problematic point of such a claim by giving an example, in which a large majority votes to enslave a small minority:

> The problem is that the minority did not agree to be bound by the results of the democratic process. However, this procedural explanation is incorrect. Suppose each member of the minority group had signed a written agreement to be so bound. Perhaps at the time they entered into the agreement, there was no prospect of a majority oppressing a minority. Sometime after they signed the agreement, a majority coalition formed and voted to enslave them. Would they be morally bound by their prior agreement to cooperate in their own enslavement? A strict proceduralist would answer yes. That is why I am not a proceduralist.[193]

The most convincing justification of democratic rights as universal human rights, according to Talbott, is that a (rights-respecting) democracy promotes appropri-

---

[189] See also Talbott, *Which Rights Should be Universal*, 112: "Human rights should be universal, because all human beings with normal cognitive, emotional, and behavioral capacities have the ability to become autonomous. In order to identify the basic human rights that should be universal, it is necessary to investigate the conditions necessary for autonomy …".
[190] Talbott, *Which Rights Should be Universal*, 139–140.
[191] See also Talbott, *Which Rights Should be Universal*, 140: "Though it is important that each person have an equal voice in democratic elections, it is hard to see how such a small amount of influence over the outcome could be seen as more than a marginal contribution to the autonomy of any individual voter."
[192] Talbott, *Which Rights Should be Universal*, 140.
[193] Talbott, *Which Rights Should be Universal*, 140.

ately distributed wellbeing and substantively just results. Democratic rights are important because they have a distinct influence on government's actions, which in turn have a fundamental impact on its citizen's life-conditions.[194] To be precise, Talbott argues that, in a rights-respecting democracy, (a) legally enforced solutions of collective action problems do not override the judgment of those it coerces but gives effect to it; (b) in combination with other human rights, democratic rights provide governments with feedback on how best to solve their citizen's collective action problems; (c) democratic rights provide reliable feedback and motivate the government to be appropriately responsive to that feedback, because the government's longevity depends on how well it promotes the wellbeing of its citizens; (d) democratic rights contribute to high stability and to an ongoing improvement of the political system; (e) the system depends on enough of their citizens developing and exercising their moral judgment; and (f) the citizens capacity for empathic understanding is required.[195] All these interdependent conditions enable Talbott to build a strong moral-instrumental argument to claim democratic rights as universal human rights. He shows democratic rights to have a fundamental mediating function structuring the relation between citizen and government in reciprocal, constructive way. Talbott points out further advantages of a rights-respecting democracy, such as stability and incremental improvement of the system, the solution of collective action problems, and the educating function of a democratic right that require the citizens to have a capacity for empathic understanding and to develop and exercise moral judgment. This allows him to shed light on the various networks of social and political relations that come along with democratic rights. Talbott emphasizes the insight that the (international) human-rights-claim for democracy is hardly one that can be understood only in procedural, (power) political terms but that it is associated with an essential society- and culture-forming overall package that depends on the inclusion of an active citizen and of rights-respecting governments of the peoples.

Talbott's flair to intertwine substantial and functional arguments shows a creative and open-angle approach to justify democratic rights. He provides a conceptualization of democracy, defining it as a rights-respecting democracy; he does not limit it to the procedural side of political institutions, to voting rights or majority decisions, but conceives it as kind of a "multi-tasking" model that involves a whole network of substantial, reciprocal relations between the citizen, the judicatory, and the government. The belief in progress and *experience* in-

---

[194] Talbott, *Which Rights Should be Universal*, 141.
[195] Talbott, *Which Rights Should be Universal*, 157–158.

duced historical human learning processes allows him to stick to credible moral claims that are justified as moral rights by reference to the past human history but open for being further developed and adapted in the future. As Reidy states:

> Talbott argues that over time human beings have discovered various universal moral truths about the nature and interests of persons and thus the ways in which they must be treated by states that claim legitimately to exercise coercive power over them. These truths are discovered through experience. They are not derived through a priori reflection. And we may always find ourselves mistaken about them. Nevertheless, they are truths about which we can be as certain as anything else we are certain of in the empirical realm. Human rights express a demand for institutions consistent with these truths.[196]

However, Talbott deals with the international dimension of human rights in a rather parsimonious way. Reidy criticizes Talbott for taking democratization of states that are not yet democratic and liberalization of states that are not yet liberal as a fundamental component on the human rights agenda.[197] Talbott's argumentation concerning the international enforcement of basic human rights is indeed unequivocal. From a moral standpoint, when human rights are being violated on a large scale and intervention could end the violations with little collateral damage, it is morally permissible for one nation to intervene in international affairs. Not explaining further details of the necessary conditions of an intervention he proposes to establish an International Criminal Court to adjudicate rights violations: "It is important that there be an international enforcement body with control over an international police force for the prevention and punishment of human rights abuse."[198] – Even though identifying such a claim to be "a direction for potential progress in the future" is controversial, such an argumentation is indeed the logical consequence of his approach.

---

[196] Reidy, "Contemporary Perspectives," 36–37.
[197] Reidy, "Contemporary Perspectives," 38.
[198] Talbott, *Which Rights Should be Universal*, 182.

3.3 Provisional appraisal of the moral conceptions

3.3.1 Insights from discussing intrinsic moral conceptions (those conceptions which derive human rights from assumptions of the basic moral nature of humans)

From the standpoint of intrinsic moral conceptions, moral and anthropological assumptions serve as reference points for evaluating whether a human right (understood to be a specific right human beings enjoy in virtue of being human) is applicable. The spectrum of arguments is very wide. According to Griffin, whereas human rights arose to protect life, liberty, and autonomy of individuals, democratic institutions arose out of the need for better decision-making within groups. For this reason, claiming an HRD is to some extent a category mistake. Nonetheless, for instrumental reasons and from a historical perspective, Griffin acknowledges that an HRD is of considerable value.

In contrast to Griffin's analysis, Nussbaum argues for a closer link between democratic rights and human nature: the ethical role of our basic capabilities, such as rationality and language, demands the exercise of practical reason, requires human affiliation, and some form of political and material control over our environment. These capabilities therefore, can also support particular claims for democratic rights, such as the right to political participation, free speech, and freedom of association. Taking the complexity of human development into account, and approaching the Rawlsian concept of public consensus, Nussbaum is not claiming a legal human right that should be implemented from top down, but she does seem to be supporting a form of soft power and development aid in order to promote capability development on a global scale. Illiterate people, for example, can hardly benefit from an HRD before having minimal education allowing them to monitor different information procedures. Sen, however, differs from Nussbaum in insisting that minimal human rights such as the right to political participation—in order to enforce fair processes—are of intrinsic value for human beings and thus have to be claimed *in addition* to capability-claims.

In the case of Forst and Benhabib, however, the *basic right to justification* is claimed to be the *right to have rights* in Arendtian style and they thereby establish the intrinsic value of democratic procedures for human life. The possibility to participate as members of equal worth in the political community is shown to be a presupposition for a human life under Forst's principle of deference: it protects personal integrity, helps to establish trust and mutual reciprocity in intersubjective relations between members of the community, and supports an internalized understanding of the value of (individual and collective) self-determination. According to these authors with a discourse theoretical background, a first (authoritative) setting of normative values such as the principle of justification or the right to have rights is legitimate despite objections of circularity. The positing of certain minimal essential values that are needed for a good human life (such as minimal political equality) is not seen as a problematic authoritative positing that overrides cultural differences if and only if it underlies an ongoing process of reflective reevaluation and if the duty to give reasons is fulfilled. Benhabib's extension of the moral claim of *a right to have rights* as a *political right to membership in a political community* to a legal claim comes close to Cohen's normative idea of membership. A similar criticism of how a human being defends him- or herself against the experience of severe injustice in the political or social community in which he or she is living in—independent of his or her membership in this particular social or political community but by virtue of his or her "membership" in the human family—surfaces again as a crucial aspect of the HRD debate. However, making a legal claim to have rights that entails *the claim of each human person to be recognized and to be protected as a legal personality by the world community*, Benhabib's formulation seems very similar to the earlier proposed human right to voice. It is important to emphasize that the world community must protect an individual right without discriminating on the basis of nationality or residence. The human right to voice must most reasonably also entail a right to exit and migration in case of unbearable social and political life conditions.

Like Forst and Benhabib, Stephan Kirste operates not from the normative principle of political equality, but from the value of legal freedom. The human right to democracy represents the guarantee for individual self-determination within a community. It is the legal condition of self-realization as it protects freedom and limits the violation of freedom. It radically involves the individual as a part of the constitution of rights and duties. Thus, Kirste sees the human right to democracy as the capstone of law, empowering and justifying human beings as authors and correctors of their rights and duties as human beings and as members of their political community. The human right to democracy is therefore something like a process right, a right to actively participate in the formation of law thanks to one's HRD-protected legal freedom.

The recognition-oriented concept of social democracy provided by Gould extends minimal-moral-autonomy- and self-determination-oriented focus of the Habermasian tradition. Her understanding of democracy goes beyond the mere formal, political aspects. With her understanding of human agency as emerging through social, relational practices, the scope of democratic measures and institutional responsibilities increases. State and society need to foster reciprocal recognition enabling people to develop their own capacities and realize life projects. Humans are viewed as social beings, as beings that are always embedded in intersubjective relations, while ideally enjoying equal agency. From a global point of view, this leads to the formulation that basic human rights are conditions to human activity and non-basic human rights are essential to people's flourishing. The requirement of equal participation in decision-making and the need for influence and rights against global decisions respectively to ones affectedness leads Gould to the comprehensive claim for global democracy, to a HRD claim. All in all, the claim for democracy matches the acknowledgement of a certain way to think worldwide human cohabitation. It assumes that human beings develop and flourish best in communities that aim to be politically and socially democratic and that are fitted out by respective institutions.

Brought together, moral intrinsic conceptions consider the individual human right to democracy (minimally in the claim of a right to have rights) to be a required component of human social life either with regard to individual capability development, gain of autonomy, protection of freedom, social trust, or self-transformation. The degree to which this claim for democratic participation is understood varies from a mere right to justification to comprehensive claims for a democratically structured society. The vast majority of authors who affirm an (individual) human right to participation also support the claim for a human right to democratic political institutions. It is essential to clearly distinguish between moral and legal human-rights-claims. Benhabib explicitly reminds us of the necessity that human rights must be defined and legitimized through their political function of guaranteeing fundamental rights *to the individual*, not through their function in international trial of strength. By this, she again emphasizes the original humanist function of human rights. The minimal form of an HRD claim as a *moral* human right to voice seems not only compatible but of basic significance for all positions cited in this section.

3.3.2 Lessons from instrumental moral conceptions

An HRD is legitimately claimed if it is a necessary instrument for realizing other human rights or fulfilling certain basic needs. According to Christiano, both the implementation of universal human rights and the world players' cooperation within the international political system depend on assured minimal conditions of minimally egalitarian democracy. He claims the moral HRD based on the normative principle of individual equality and underlines it by his use of empirical findings that are meant to prove the positive effects of democratic government on both domestic and international level. As Beitz and others have pointed out, most scholars attach little importance to the negative effects of democratization as well as the challenge of a practical implementation of an HRD. Apart from Christiano's noticeable tendency to liberal democratic optimism, he introduces important empirical aspects to highlight the empirical correlation between human rights and democracy against a political background. His argumentation adds the empirical basis to support the abstract Habermasian thesis of equiprimordiality of human rights and democracy.

Besson argues systematically for a crossover between the moral, the political, and the legal dimensions of human rights and democracy. She further argues for the mutual reinforcement between international *demoi-cracy* and the international legal right to democracy. According to Besson, as soon as democratic principles organize the international organization and collaboration between actors, a legal human right to democracy must necessarily follow. Interestingly, she says that the HRD is already part of the existing human rights codex (Article III of the Declaration of the Rights of Man and of the Citizen, Article 21 of the Universal Declaration of Human Rights, Article 25 of the International Covenant on Civil and Political Rights), because, in these articles, participation and rights are based on citizenship. These rights do not therefore cover a minimal human right to (democratic) voice that a human being has independent of his or her nationality.

Dahl argues against the possibility of democratic international institutions by showing that the particular advantages afforded the citizens by a democratic procedural system depend, for instance, on the citizens' minimal substantial identification and understanding of the political matter. The complexity of international affairs and the difficulty to agree on a global public good both undermine the influence of individual democratic participation. Therefore, according to Dahl, the correlation postulated by Besson between an international legal (human) right to democracy and international *demoi-cracy* is not a necessary one. In addition, Dahl's argumentation seems to support the claim for an individual right to democratic participation: His argument promotes democracy straight forwardly by pointing out that it is the best form of government to protect personal autonomy, to account for intrinsic equality of humans and to ensure the principle of equal consideration of interest.

Distancing himself from the necessary linkage between human rights and democracy, Arneson claims that the moral right to democracy should not be included among basic moral rights, as the exercise of the vote is considered to be an exercise of power. He prioritizes the promotion of intrinsic individual rights as criterion for a just society. The decision for a specific governmental form needs to be evaluated by the criterion of how well it serves to enforce individual rights. Rejecting the assumption of democratic procedures as necessarily just procedures, he does "not see any reason at all to accept the claim that only choice of democracy can express the idea that persons have equal basic moral status."[199] However, if moral evaluation and judgments are decisive, Arneson leaves open to whom the legitimate moral authority is owned, and how the moral status and standards are defined and validated.

Whereas Dahl includes the premise of unquestioned intrinsic value of autonomy in his instrumental argument for democratic government, Miller avoids any reference to such ("metaphysical" or intrinsic) moral concepts. According to Miller's human-needs-oriented approach, the *practical agreement* regarding human rights is crucial to their legitimation. Human rights are defined as rights that serve to guarantee basic human needs. The latter are identified by a so-called *humanitarian strategy* and characterized by a priority of physical, material needs that are human rights relevant. According to Miller, a human right to democratic institutions falls out of the territory of urgent human rights because the human rights value of democratic institutions is dependent from their quality and implementation. Miller endorses "some form" of a human right to participation understood as the right to vote that enables the right-holder to maintain "the power to check those who make political decisions."[200]

Against this, Talbott includes the HRD, understood as a complex of political rights, including democratic rights and an independent judiciary to enforce the entire package of rights, in his list of nine basic human rights. Talbott's strongest argument for the HRD states that a rights-respecting democracy promotes appropriately distributed wellbeing, and promotes substantively just results. Adding the mediating function that democratic rights play between citizens and governments, he argues for a universal HRD against the background of the historical-social process of moral learning.

Scrutinizing the moral instrumental conceptions shows that they mostly pull out their instrumental value of human rights because of the beforehand stated conception of a good life, of certain (self-evidently assumed) human values or needs. Unlike the moral intrinsic conceptions they have to provide less exhaustive derivations of such normative goals, as they do not aim to prove an intrinsic relation between such values and the HRD-claim but determine them respectively to their basic assumptions. Despite considerable differences in argumentation, apart from Arnson's and Miller's approaches (which seems to allow a right to voice claim only in case of physical or material harm), the minimal democratic claim to voice remains unchallenged.

---

199 Arneson, "Debate," 131.
200 Miller, *"Is there a Human Right to Democracy?,"* 15.

4 An alternative perspective on the human right to democracy

4.1 Post analysis: key findings summarized

The human right to democracy has inspired a growing body of scholarship. Representing human rights from a moral perspective, the human right to democracy has been argued for as a precondition for living a decent and self-determined life in political societies. The gradual differences between moral positions are mirrored by the extent of each concrete human right to democracy claim or its rejection. Whereas authors such as Christiano argue for worldwide institutional implementation of minimal egalitarian democracy, authors like Miller limit their claim on the basic human right to political participation. In contrast to the moral positions argued for from the viewpoint of a human being with needs, capacities and dignity, the political positions argue against a human right to democratic institutions with a view to the requirements and limits of international political action taking and collaboration.

The adaption of the fourfold thematic map helped to analyze and compare the contemporary arguments for or against a HRD and to get a well-structured overview of the various authors' positions. The distinction between moral and political rationales classifies an approach as a *political* one, on the one hand, if the claim or rejection of the HRD is justified by emphasizing either reasons concerning the logic and optimization of the existent supranational system, or by emphasizing general political normative aims (such as the right of a political community to collective self-determination, to minimal social justice, or, more generally, to peace). Conceptions classified as *moral* ones, on the other hand, start their reasoning from the bottom up, as it were, and ask why a HRD can or cannot be claimed from the moral standpoint of any reasonable human being. Methodologically, the two rationales have been further divided according to either their intrinsic or instrumental form of argumentation. Hence, the distinction of four categories of human rights conceptions led to four different possible answers to the HRD question. Thus, I distinguished between the categories of normative political conceptions, instrumental political conceptions, intrinsic moral conceptions, and instrumental moral conceptions. *Normative political conceptions* emphasize normative political ideals and principles concerning the welfare of societies such as justice, equality, popular sovereignty or collective self-determination. They aim at a legitimate and just social and political order. Authors argue for or against a HRD by examining if democratic rights or institutions are an intrinsically valuable precondition to realize normative political principles and ideals. Joshua Cohen's idea of membership and philosophical contributions from Alyssa R. Bernstein, Matthew Lister and David A. Reidy have been discussed under this heading. *Instrumental political conceptions* emphasize the role that human rights play in international relations as political and public instruments. Partisans of this approach take empirical reasons into "normative" consideration and define legitimacy as the practical applicability and efficiency of human rights in international political contexts. The justification of a HRD claim depends on its value for strategic, political goals of the international community, for example, as a legitimate instrument to impose sanctions on regimes that violate other human rights. Discussed under the heading of instrumental political conceptions, Charles Beitz's rejection of a HRD provided a major contribution to the debate. It stands in contrast to the contribution of Allan Buchanan who argued for minimal democracy as a legitimate claim. *Intrinsic moral conceptions* derive human rights from assumptions concerning human nature, general human conditions, capabilities and needs. Correspondingly, they are postulated to protect essential human features (such as particular understandings of human dignity) and to enable the unfolding of individuals' potentials and capabilities by ensuring the satisfaction of basic claims and needs. Only if it can be shown that the right to democracy is a right that each human has simply in virtue of being a human being, and as a right that guarantees human dignity, the claim equates a justified *human rights* claim. Several, in fact most, of the debate's authors have been classified under the heading of intrinsic moral conceptions. Contributions from moral philosopher James Griffin, capability-philosophers such as Martha Nussbaum and Amartya Sen, critical theorists such as Rainer Forst and Seyla Benhabib, but also the social philosopher Carol C. Gould and Stephan Kirste as a philosopher of law enriched a diversified discussion. *Instrumental moral conceptions* argue, as do intrinsic moral conceptions, from the wellbeing and vulnerability of individuals. Disparaging of intrinsic moral conceptions, they emphasize the contingency of human rights due to their practical, historical, and political constructiveness. Human rights are seen as instruments to protect humans from injuries, which are defined as human rights violations. The justification of a HRD claim proves that the HRD is necessary to guarantee other human rights. Several authors team up under the heading of instrumental moral conceptions headed by Thomas Christiano, Samantha Besson, and Richard J. Arneson. Robert Dahl, David Miller, and William Talbott are listed in this category as well, whereas they could alternatively be construed as offering moral intrinsic contributions, as their thoughts include major borrowings from intrinsic moral argumentation.

My initial desire in approaching this topic was simply to understand and map out the different voices partaking in this debate. Certainly, the entanglement of moral, political and legal aspects complicates the comparative discussion of philosophical approaches that provide answers to the question whether there should be a human right to democracy. Additionally, from a methodical standpoint, few authors can be neatly classified into the fourfold scheme. Some authors such as Martha Nussbaum or James Griffin have been selected as contributors to the debate not because they provide a particular contribution to the HRD debate but for providing enough HRD related thinking in their human rights theories to derive a HRD position. The selection of these authors has been made to point out how the differences in human rights theories matter and get reflected in the normative evaluation about whether there should be a human right to democracy. In general, however, the fourfold classification and its adaption to several human rights conceptions reveal that the divergences concerning content are narrower than were to be expected.

Despite the lack of consensus among authors, the real controversies between them tend to concentrate on practical, political matters of implementation. In contrast to a relative uniformity in contra arguments, the pro arguments are highly varied. The core issue of whether a moral human right to democracy should be claimed—that is, abstracting from factual worldwide conditions—appears far less controversial. None of the objections against the HRD claim, for instance, amounts to an objection to democracy as such. Most authors who reject the human right to democratic institutions implicitly or even explicitly affirm democratic principles and democracy's various normative criteria. This finding has important implications for distinguishing between moral, legal, and political dimensions when theorizing the HRD. Whereas the moral claim for an (individual) human right to democratic participation is affirmed by the majority of authors in at least some minimal sense of recourse—a right every individual should possess in the face of injustice inflicted by the community, including a right to dissent from collective decisions—the legal and political claim for a human right to political democratic institutions is far more problematic. I believe that it is often taken for granted that moral human rights must be thought as necessarily congruent with legal human rights, but this should be questioned. It is important to state well-reflected moral human rights claims that serve as a point of orientation for philosophical and political discussions, even if the contemporary world situation makes it impossible to implement legal rights that would be identical to the ideal moral rights. The common distinction between basic and non-basic human rights converges partly with the distinction between moral rights and legal rights. That is to say, first, that the claim for basic rights (which are of such urgency that violations result in legitimate international intervention) can be defined as moral rights that already have their one-to-one legal equivalents. Second, the claim for non-basic human rights can be conceptualized as moral rights of which the universal implementation in political and legal context is principally required but must be targeted in a long-term development process.

The key aspects of this book's argumentation can be summarized in a dialectical triad as follows. First, it was shown how moral conceptions value personhood and human needs, interests and capabilities to derive human rights. But this humanist emphasis is at odds with practical, political conceptions. Second, in due consideration of the arguments from the political conceptions, the claim of a comprehensive human right to democracy is ill advised from a contemporary, human, moral standpoint. Third, as I will elaborate at length in the last sections of this chapter, the common denominator of a *human right to voice* can be justified from a moral human standpoint but also from a political standpoint—which seems compatible with the Rawlsian requirement of the consultation hierarchy in decent countries. Further research is needed to establish and account for the precise boundaries between moral and legal rights in general, and, in particular, between a human right enabling individual (democratic) voice and a human right to democratic institutions. However, the widespread rejection of a human right to democratic institutions should not lead us to the conclusion that the legal, political claim for a human right to voice is also necessarily unobtainable. On the contrary, the extraction of the general insight, that the philosophical affirmation of the HRD, understood as a moral human right to voice, is hardly controversial, should be considered to be of fundamental political and symbolical value. To bring this extended discussion of the human right to democracy debate to a close, it is first of all necessary to specify the possible content and limits of a human right to voice. If such a right has to be morally justified and feasible from an international political standpoint, what does it include?

4.2 An alternative view: the human right to voice

4.2.1 The moral and social philosophical justification of a human right to voice

The human right to voice can be defined as a right that secures the individual political right to complain, or organize to complain or to protest if, for example, the individual becomes endangered or harmed within the society it is living in. The critique of Cohen's normative idea of membership helped to elaborate the way in which the human right to voice assigns the individual the moral and political competence and authorization to present basic interests, rights and needs in form of a communicative and public act in his or her society. Cohen's idea of membership includes an individual equal right to political participation but is not distinct enough to justify the individual member's right to be heard and protected from unjust harm and severe repression that his or her own membership community exercises upon him/her. This diagnosis helped in filtering out the right to voice representing the basic normative core of the human right to democracy. It justifies dissent and protest against the society's denial of individual rights, against injustice or harm experienced or not prevented through one's own political government. Claiming a right to voice, e. g. to be heard, recognized and supported in political needs and experiences of repression in one's own society (be it at home, in education or at the workplace) cannot be justified through the normative argument of collective self-determination by which Cohen justifies the individual right to inclusion. According to this view, the right to dissent from and appeal to collective decisions is justified only against the assumption of a shared conception of the society's common good.

Prima facie, the above stated claims of a human right to voice could be summarized under the heading of individual self-determination as claimed by Rainer Forst, Seila Benhabib, and Stephan Kirste. But even if the right to voice clearly can be seen in relation to the generally more comprehensive claim for political self-determination and moral autonomy, its function is narrower. What the human right to voice protects is a minimal realm of moral and social freedom,[1] the integrity of the individual's internal liberty to stand up for herself and her life plan despite standing in an asymmetrical social or political relation to the powerful authority or to the majority. Prior to the normative claim for political equality, the normative core of the human right to voice (which is to say: its intrinsic justification from a moral human standpoint), is the irrevocable claim of minimal *self-disposability* [*Selbstverfügbarkeit*] within the social and political community one is living in. Thus, even if not necessarily protecting the *physical* vulnerability of human beings, its instrumental function is, on the one hand, to protect personal integrity by guaranteeing minimal freedom to articulate one's interests and needs. Apart from protecting the 'sender's' freedom of speech, the human right to voice expresses the requirement of a 'receiver'-side that adequately responds to the particular appeal. Thus, on the other hand, the human right to voice emphasizes the requirement of any successful intersubjective communication act by pointing out the necessity to provide a receiver-side to the sender, such as a representative or public hearing and response to the appeals of singu-

---

[1] Axel Honneth introduces the notion of social freedom in Hegelian footsteps, in: Axel Honneth, *Freedom's Right: The Social Foundations of Democratic Life* (Cambridge: Polity, 2014).

lar members. From an existential point of view, the human right to voice therefore reflects the paradigm of intersubjectivity, stating that human development and behavior can only be understood and transformed in the context of relatedness, in a context where a claim or action find an adequate response. Thus, the human right to voice can be seen as a basic institution of recognition protecting and representing the individual's social and juridical freedom to engage in active self-realization by means of participation in speech-acts. From a hermeneutical philosophical perspective, Paul Ricoeur describes the underlying need to be recognized as a "speaking subject" in his "phenomenology of the capable human being,"[2] with a reference to the theory of speech acts.

> It is the fact that to speak, following the well-known saying of J.L. Austin, is "to do things with words." By launching the idea of capacity by way of being able to say things, we confer on the notion of human action the extension that justifies the characterization of the self as the capable human being recognizing himself in his capabilities.[3]

Ricoeur describes interlocutory situations as the locus where the self-designation of the speaking subject is produced, "where the reflexivity is combined with otherness." The existential relevance of discourse, of having a voice and being heard by others, is represented by the insight that any speech pronounced by someone is a speech act addressed to someone else, often even a response to a call from others: "The structure of question and answer thus constitute the basic structure of discourse, in implicating the speaker and the interlocutor."[4] Applied to the human right to voice discussion, the denial of a human right to voice is a radical denial of discourse, which —according to Ricoeur—equals the denial of the recognition as a capable human being. Subsequently, this denial reduces the individual's scope of action, extends to a denial of accountability, makes it impossible for the human agent to undertake responsibilities, and impairs personal and collective identity formation.[5]

Less focused on the speech act dimension but more to the social philosophical side, Axel Honneth's recognition theory provides relevant reasons for the moral and psychological significance of intersubjective and juridical recognition of someone's voice for a stable positive self-relation, for the relation to the other and for reasonable dealing with the social and political collective. In his more

---

[2] Paul Ricoeur, *The Course of Recognition* (Cambridge: Harvard University Press, 2005), 89–109.
[3] Ricoeur, *The Course of Recognition*, 94.
[4] Ricoeur, *The Course of Recognition*, 96.
[5] Ricoeur, *The Course of Recognition*, 104–109.

recent analysis in *Freedom's Right*,[6] these relational competences of the subject are crucial with regard to the formation of ethical life in a democratic society. From a psychological standpoint, being guaranteed hearing and response meets the basic personal need to experience self-efficacy in social relations. Having a voice frees one from invisibility, and by this, it also becomes the source of personal responsibility. The opportunity to articulate and defend one's particular self-understanding is a necessary condition to individuate and to live free from harm and danger within a community.

Honneth's conception of recognition is based on the assumption that the intersubjective dynamics of recognition structure the private and the public communities, and that reciprocal recognition is vital for the individuals development of capabilities and its individuation. The development of human capabilities and of social and moral imputability requires a minimal satisfaction of individual needs for recognition. Relations of recognition are necessary conditions for moral subjectivity, fostering practical relations-to-self in the form of self-confidence, self-respect, and self-esteem.[7] These three positive attitudes correspond with the three levels of recognition in the theoretical model: The first form of recognition is developed in primary relationships (love, friendship), the second one is experienced in legal relations (rights), and the third one in once community of value (solidarity).[8] Communicative self-expression, self-reliant negation and affirmation, and effective participation in the discourse about one's own needs and life conditions are relevant at all three levels of recognition. However, in our human rights context, they seem of particular importance at the second level. Referring to G.H. Mead, Honneth describes the development of cognitive respect of a person who has learned to view himself or herself from the perspective of a generalized other as the particular self-understanding of a legal person. In the process of becoming a socially accepted member of one's community the person learns to appropriate the social norms of the generalized other by way of an internalization of the others normative attitudes and the norms of cooperation.[9] In addition to the internalized insight into the logic of rights and obligations, reciprocal recognition and responsibilities in a community, a functional system of legal recognition must be based on the knowledge of secured long term communal life. The generally valid structure of rights and obligations en-

---

6 Axel Honneth, *Freedom's right: the social foundations of democratic life* (Cambridge: Polity, 2014).
7 Axel Honneth, *The Struggle for Recognition: The Moral Grammar of Social Conflicts*, trans. Joel Anderson (Cambridge: Polity Press, 1996), ch. 5.
8 Honneth, *The Struggle for Recognition: The Moral Grammar of Social Conflicts*, 129.
9 Honneth, *The Struggle for Recognition: The Moral Grammar of Social Conflicts*, 79.

sures at the same time a private space in which the individual can develop and aim for his own conception of the good life. The experience of being recognized as a legal person allows the individual to adopt a positive attitude towards herself: The conferral of rights comes down to the attribution of personal properties accounting for the individual's moral accountability. The consequences, which violations of legal status can have on the individual's self-understanding are described as a deprivation of self-respect:

> For the individual, having socially valid rights-claims denied signifies a violation of the intersubjective expectation to be recognized as a subject capable of forming moral judgements. To this extent, the experience of this type of disrespect typically brings with it a loss of self-respect, of the ability to relate to oneself as a legally equal interaction partner with all fellow humans.[10]

The denigration and exclusion from the legal community further leads to the loss of self-esteem as the individual can no more refer to himself as an equally entitled fellow being. The restriction of personal freedom that a subject experiences through the denial of legal recognition and participation leads not just to a constraint of capable action but to an isolating constraint of possible social interaction and social (intersubjective) freedom.[11] The concept of social freedom represents the Hegelian idea that self-awareness is attained only by regarding the other as other. Further differentiated as a concept to normatively reconstruct the spheres of market and public democratic life, concerning the private sphere social freedom stands for the experience of "being with oneself in the other".[12] This idea of social freedom is "rooted in a conception of social institutions in which subjects can grasp each other as the other of their own selves".[13] In this sense, as a "social institution" the human right to voice protects more than the individual freedom and political participation. Standing for the idea that realization of individual (reflexive) freedom depends on a social and political reality in which reciprocal and complementary deliberation and equal say are guaranteed, it represents a basic institution for the realization of social freedom.[14] In Honneth's theory of democratic ethical life[15] (*demokratische Sittlichkeit*), the function of both liberties and social rights on the one hand, and polit-

---

10 Honneth, *The Struggle for Recognition: The Moral Grammar of Social Conflicts*, 133 f.
11 Honneth, *Freedom's Right*, 42 f.
12 Honneth, *Freedom's Right*, 44.
13 Honneth, *Freedom's Right*, 44.
14 Honneth, *Freedom's Right*, ch. 3.
15 Honneth, *Freedom's right*.

ical rights (voting rights, right to assemble, and to form associations[16]) on the other hand, is shown to be crucial for the citizen as an opportunity to identify with the society and to form a shared we-perspective as a basis for democratic solidarity.

> After all, political rights necessarily involve an activity that can only be carried out in cooperation, or at least in exchange, with all other fellow legal subjects. The significance of the difference between liberties and social rights of participation on the one hand, and political rights of participation on the other hand, is not only empirical but also conceptual: The first two categories of rights can only be appropriately understood and implemented if individuals use them to form a private "I", while the third category of rights must be viewed as an invitation to engage in civil activity and thus in the formation of a common will.[17]

In its reading as a moral human right, the right to voice expresses first of all a basic individual and social liberty. However, understood as a legal, political claim, it also represents a political right to participation. By this twofold function, the human right to voice symbolizes the bridge between freedom and intersubjective recognition on the basis of which democratic ethical life can only become realized in a collective. Ethical life requires the subjects shared self-understanding that recognition of individual differences and pluralism is built on the basis of a common understanding of rights but also on its reference to the societies general moral value system. The latter allows social identification and solidarity, but also becomes the reference point for citizens or groups to dissent from. On the one hand, the idea of a right to voice represents the freedom right to stand up for one's individual interests and values in a social and political context, on the other hand, the dependence of a right to voice from being heard through another represents the basic social, communal recognition that this right guarantees. If and only if the smallest entity that shapes democracy, the individual, has a voice, the minimal condition for the establishment of democratic life praxis is fulfilled. Against this background, human right to voice can be seen as a substantial component in realizing democratic ethical life.

In a nutshell, both Honneth and Ricoeur link the ethical requirement to recognize a human being's "voice" to the personal development of identity, capabilities, responsibility, and finally, by both citing Joel Feinberg, to human dignity: "What is called 'human dignity' may simply be the recognizable capacity to assert claims."[18] With a view to the well-known objection of culturally relative

---

16 Honneth, *Freedom's Right*, 259.
17 Honneth, *Freedom's Right*, 79.
18 Joel Feinberg, *Rights, Justice, and the Bounds of Liberty: Essays in Social Philosophy* (Princeton, N.J.: Princeton University Press, 1980).

human rights values, one could ask again whether the claim for a human right to voice borrows from a too strong Western liberal ideal of moral autonomy and individual self-determination. I believe that the minimal content of "moral autonomy" that we have to proclaim for a human right to voice guaranteeing the assertion of individual claims in a (repressive) social environment does not overstretch the limits of human rights' universalizability. There is no moral judgment involved against those individual members of a society that for example consciously accept the social repression they face because of their low status within the caste system for religious reasons. But for those humans who have a self-understanding that differs from their society's understanding of the good (entailing a reference to moral autonomy), and who cannot live according to it without severely suffering in psychic, social or physical life, the right to voice is demanded.

Several examples falling under area of responsibility of the enforcers of a human right to voice can be given, each showing the high complexity and difficulty to implement such a moral rights idea under given world political circumstances. Nevertheless, they help to shine a light on fundamental and unaccounted for injustices on individual level that should be acknowledged from a substantial human rights standpoint and for which perception the consciousness of the international human rights community should increase. From a human rights standpoint, where the nation-state is not capable or willing to protect the individual against severe injustice, the international community's responsibility to support the particular individual arises.

Let me first take up the example of forced marriage. Imagine the example of a young woman born in an orthodox family in a non-secular and conservatively religious state who identifies herself with a strong value of personal autonomy and self-determination. Despite her cultural identity and connectedness to her family and society, her "voice" saying that she wants to choose her own partner for a lifetime is not heard by her family. She tries to argue reasonably for her rights but her voice as a woman is given less force and her father and uncles interpret her repugnance as a sign of immodesty and immaturity. In her local environment, there are no approachable mediators or ombudsmen who could support her in this distress. To whom could she possibly make an appeal to be heard in her concerns? Will she flee her village hoping for another life abroad? Will she be trapped and punished, or become a feminist activist in a more open environment? Will she surrender to the values of her patriarchs and finally raise her daughter in the same ancient spirit? Will she surrender to a forced marriage while building up a secret network of local women that aim for freedom rights? The reader can easily imagine how this story ends.

Another possible case falling under the jurisdiction of a human right to voice would be the freshman worker in a factory in a poor country who learns that several of his co-workers get sick and die within a work period of few years in the same factory. Researching and inquiring among his experienced colleges, the father of three children finds out that the glue the workers are required to use by the overseers must contain highly poisonous ingredients. Trying to complain at his superiors, they advise him to either work on without complaining, or to quit the job and promise absolute discreetness about his findings. Threatened to not be sure of his own and his family's life again if not surrendering to one of the given ultimate options, the worker finds himself in a life threatening dilemma. Trying to appeal to national work agencies, he finds himself standing in front of closed doors. Are there real other options then the ultimate ones, and to whom could he possibly make an appeal to be heard in his concerns? Will he try to organize a protest with his co-workers despite knowing that he puts his and their life in danger? Will he continue working in the factory silently because he decides it to be more important to sustain his family and to enable his kids a better education than to secure his own health?

To finish with a third example, imagine a history teacher in a country ruled by despotism. The teacher is constrained to teach the history of his country's relation to neighbor states according a national curriculum. He knows that the textbooks contain ideologically biased propaganda and rabble-rousing and derogatory exposition of the neighbors. Aware that in the long term he helps to mobilize a new generation of pupils for the next war against these neighboring countries, he wants to refuse teaching counterfactual stories. However, his experience prooves that he will be prosecuted for disobedience by the state as soon as he implements his decision publicly. Again, we can ask what options the teacher has to escape the personal dilemma. To whom can he appeal for support and protection? Does he decide to stand up for his belief despite the risk to spend a lifetime in prison? Does he consider going into hiding and adopting a new identity in the underground? Does he consider speaking up in public or rather emigrating to a country respecting his freedom rights?

We can only speculate about the fate of these individuals. Of course, we could continue with several more examples where the lack of voice represents a severe restriction to basic political and individual freedoms. Already these few examples imply how complex and illusionary it seems to practically provide being heard and supported to all these myriads of individuals worldwide whose life situations would benefit from human rights protection. The questions in what form and to what extent an institutionalized agency of the international community could take over responsibility over time and support the individual in particular circumstances are a different matter to which no panacea is available. Besides the morally justified claim of a repressed individual stand antagonist political interests, and diplomatic relations in practice. Despite these difficulties, and under the widely shared hope for incremental democratic development minimally in decent countries, naming these 'taboo' human rights issues on individual level seems fair. As I already pointed out, the international political impracticality of supporting the individual within the problematically acting country throws up the question of whether the international community would have to support the exit option. At this point, Albert O. Hirschman's conceptual and sociological contribution to the human right to voice idea from *Exit, Voice, and Loyalty*[19] and the conceptual revision he gave in *Exit, Voice, and the Fate of the German Democratic Republic*[20] provides an attractive endorsement. In the course of reconstructing Hirschman's concept of voice it becomes obvious that the exit option correlates or – in a strong interpretation: co-emerges – with the (denied) voice option. The discussion about a human right to voice will be shown to transport the follow-up question of a right to exit. According to Warren's subsequent analysis,[21] exit represents a political course of action with significant democratic potential. To begin with the reconstruction, Hirschman's use of the concept "voice" that inspired the idea of a "human right to voice" is summarized.

4.2.2 Voice and exit in Albert O. Hirschman's footsteps

All in all, my adaption of Hirschman's analytical categories of voice and exit understands them as a template structuring and helping to extrapolate the human rights relevance of voice, but also shining a light on the exit option as a possible co- or complementary right to the right to voice. In a political process, as Hirschman points out, having a voice to articulate one's protest and to be heard from the responsible political authorities can operate as a substitute for the use of the exit option. This link is of contemporary importance for the reflection about the contemporary migration challenges, itself clearly being one of the empirical fields in which both the human right to voice and the exit option become live options. In general and especially concerned about conceiving the content and

---

19 Albert O. Hirschman, *Exit, Voice, and Loyalty: Responses to Decline in Firms, Organizations, and States* (Cambridge, Mass.: Harvard University Press, 1970).
20 Hirschman, "Exit, Voice, and the Fate of the German Democratic Republic," 45(02) *World Politics* (1993): 173–202.
21 Mark E. Warren, "Voting with Your Feet: Exit-Based Empowerment in Democratic Theory," 105 *American Political Science Review* (2011): 683–701, doi:10.1017/S0003055411000323.

limits of a human right to voice, Hirschman's template is used primarily as a structuring perspective on the logic of political participation within in the context of political or social repression. Tolerating and encouraging the study of the particular, contextual relationship between voice and exit against the background of the assumption that manifold relationships between the two logics are per se possible, the template's openness and simplicity matches this purpose.

Starting from Hirschman's thoughts, "the voice option" is originally introduced as one of two indicators in economic organization theory. The "exit option" represents the second indicator. Outgoing from his analysis focused on economics and management processes, Hirschman adapts the findings as one way to understand wider political participation processes. In the course of his examination of "exit and voice" lasting from the late 1960ties to the early 1990ies, he discusses the relation between these two forms of protest of customers against a firm or of citizens against their repressive governments in several ways. Whereas in his earlier writings[22] exit and voice are discussed as two 'alternative routes' in customers' reaction to deterioration in a firm or another type of organization, revised and to particular contexts extended ways of interplay between exit and voice become elaborated in his later work.[23]

To understand Hirschman's use of the concepts of voice and exit, his monograph *Exit, Voice, and Loyalty* (1970) provides a good starting point. Hirschman describes therein how in case of deterioration in performance of a firm, the structural deterioration is typically accompanied by an absolute or comparative deterioration of the quality of the product or service provided. According to Hirschman, there are two options the customers can choose to express their dissatisfaction with the deterioration of product or service quality. First, the exit option lies in the customers' choice to stop buying the firm's products or to quit their membership in the organization. Second, the voice option lies in the customers or organization's members' expression of dissatisfaction either directly confronting the management or responsible agency, or through "general protest addressed to anyone who cares to listen."[24] Initially, Hirschman understands exit as an economic, and voice as a political mechanism. Pointing out the potential of reciprocity of both concepts, he intends to demonstrate the usefulness of economic concepts to political scientists and the usefulness of political concepts to economists. Particularly in his later work, both the voice but also the exit option in form of emigration are described as options individuals and

---

[22] Hirschman, *Exit, Voice, and Loyalty*, ch. 1.
[23] Hirschman, "Exit, Voice, and the Fate of the German Democratic Republic."
[24] Hirschman, *Exit, Voice, and Loyalty*, 4.

groups make use of in the political sphere of their societies. Whereas the exit option is described as a *private* and typically silent decision and activity of an individual that leaves the country to find a more satisfactory environment, the voice option is described as typically a *public* activity:

> Though it [the voice option] does not indispensably require organization, action in concert with others, delegation, and all the other features of collective action, it thrives on it.[25]

The voice option can be executed from a singular human standpoint but always requires a recipient of one's message and a sufficient response. Joined by fellow travelers, it can also be used to organize a collective movement, for example in using petitions or demonstrations. If the right of voice as a public option is categorically denied, the private decision to exit the country is often the standing to reason way out of a repressive life situation. Criticizing Hirschman's tenuous discussion of exit as a democratic response, Mark E. Warren emphasizes the exit-based empowerment of the individual in claiming its connection to two basic norms of democratic theory, the non-domination principle and the all-affected principle. The principle of non-domination contends that individuals should not be subject to domination but have political, economic, and social empowerments sufficient for them to avoid relations of domination and to exercise individual autonomy. The all-affected principle refers to the claim of self-determination and states that those who are potentially affected by collective decisions should have the opportunity to influence those decisions.[26] The implementation of these principles requires the individual's right to voice and a guarantee to be heard. If voice is denied, exit can function as a key mechanism in breaking a relationship of domination or generating attentiveness for social injustices in an organization or under a political regime. Therefore, as an alternative to rights-based inclusion, exit provides the "communicative feature" of a signal under circumstances in which voice is denied.[27] Thus, exit as a form of political action carries communicative content without necessarily carrying linguistic content. The metaphor of "voting with your feet" represents this non-verbal communicative act in an apt way. Apart from the neglect of exit's communicative function, Warren argues that Hirschman's "voice-monopoly-model" underestimates the role exit plays in terms of power: Exit may function to change asymmetrical relationships of power into symmetrical relationships of choice, at least if the individual has an alternative relationship option (for example an unsatisfied em-

---

25 Hirschman, "Exit, Voice, and the Fate of the German Democratic Republic," 194.
26 Warren, "Voting with Your Feet: Exit-Based Empowerment in Democratic Theory," 687.
27 Warren, "Voting with Your Feet: Exit-Based Empowerment in Democratic Theory," 684.

ployee or customer quitting his firm and choosing a new business). This objection points out the important distinction between exit understood as an option that benefits people exiting and between exit as a strategic means that can have an effect of changing the unjust structure in a country or organization for the better. Whereas the first option seems primary for our thinking about exit in the human rights context, the second option requests a further study of political dynamics that might follow the utilization of the exit option.

Initially rejecting the assumption of a pre-established harmony between exit and voice, and in contrast following the idea that "they often work at cross-purpose and tend to undermine each other, in particular with exit undermining voice," Hirschman himself later reformulates the relation between exit and voice in Warren's direction. He uses the metaphor of a "basic seesaw pattern," which is characterized by a "hydraulic" model illustrating how "deterioration generates the pressure of discontent, which will be channeled into voice or exit; the more pressure escapes through exit, the less is available to foment voice."[28] In the course of studying the events of 1989 in the GDR, he further extends the possible interplay of the mechanisms in the political field in demonstrating that exit (out-migration) and voice (protest demonstrations against the regime) can reinforce each other in particular situations, and work in tandem. Identifying exit and voice as two basic complementary ingredients of democratic freedom, he describes them now as "on the whole enlarged or restricted jointly" in a political process.[29] Depending on the momentous political and social constellation, "exit can cooperate with voice, voice can emerge from exit, and exit can reinforce voice."[30] From Hirschman's sociological and economical thoughts about exit and voice, enriched by Warren's revaluation of the democratic potential of exit, a bridge can be built back to the philosophical, Rawlsian idea of a consultation hierarchy in *The Law of Peoples*,[31] and the therein noticed right to emigration. Let me therefore take a last twist that leads us back to the "Rawlsian shadow" we already discussed at the very beginning of the book. The idea of the consultation hierarchy in decent countries complementing the Rawlsian human rights theory is used as a perspective from which the idea of a human right to voice can be critically discussed.

---

28 Hirschman, "Exit, Voice, and the Fate of the German Democratic Republic," 176.
29 Hirschman, "Exit, Voice, and the Fate of the German Democratic Republic," 177.
30 Hirschman, "Exit, Voice, and the Fate of the German Democratic Republic," 202.
31 Rawls, *The Law of Peoples* (Cambridge, Mass.: Harvard University Press, 2002).

4.2.3 The human right to voice under an international, political philosophical viewpoint: is Rawls's consultation hierarchy a critique of the idea of a human right to voice?

Discussing the human right to voice requires considering the criterion of a consultation hierarchy Rawls establishes as a second requirement for decent countries in *The Law of Peoples*. Besides the criterion that a decent society's system of law needs to be guided by a common good idea of justice, he insists that the legal system of a decent hierarchical people must contain a decent consultation hierarchy.[32] This consultation hierarchy is described as a basic structure of the society that must "include a family of representative bodies whose role in the hierarchy is to take part in an established procedure of consultation and to look after what the people's common good idea of justice regards as the important interest of all members of the people."[33] Prima facie, the idea of a consultation hierarchy seems close to the idea of a human right to voice, since it states that each person belongs to a group represented by a body in the consultation hierarchy, and each person engages in distinctive activities and plays a certain role in the overall scheme of cooperation. Even closer to the idea of a human right to voice, Rawls states that persons as members of associations, corporations, and estates have the right to express political dissent at some point of the procedure of consultation (often at the state of selecting a groups representatives): "the government has an obligation to take a group's dissent seriously and to give a conscientious reply."[34]

> It is necessary and important that different voices be heard, because judges' and other officials' sincere belief in the justice of the legal system must include respect for the possibility of dissent. Judges and other officials must be willing to address objections. They cannot refuse to listen, charging that the dissenters are incompetent and unable to understand, for then we would have not a decent consultation hierarchy, but a paternalistic regime. Moreover, should the judges and other officials listen, the dissenters are not required to accept the answer given to them; they may renew their protest, provided they explain why they are still dissatisfied, and their explanation in turn ought to receive a further and fuller reply. Dissent expresses a form of public protest and is permissible provided it stays within the basic framework of the common good idea of justice.[35]

---

[32] Rawls, *The Law of Peoples*, 71.
[33] Rawls, *The Law of Peoples*, 71.
[34] Rawls, *The Law of Peoples*, 72.
[35] Rawls, *The Law of Peoples*, 72.

Although the actors of Rawls's international theory are peoples, not individuals, he justifies the necessity and importance of different voices to be heard significantly by referring to the individual dissenters' moral entitlement to ask for reasons and justification.

> Although all persons in a decent hierarchical society are not regarded as free and equal citizens, nor as separate individuals deserving equal representation (according to the maxim: one citizen, one vote), they are seen as decent and rational and as capable of moral learning as recognized in their society.[36]

Although the argument focuses on people in decent countries, the general concept of the person is hardly differently conceptualized for persons in outlaw states, societies burdened by unfavorable conditions, or societies that are benevolent absolutisms. Rawls describes just the latter as not being well ordered because their members are denied a meaningful role in making political decisions.[37] The Rawlsian vision entails that the Law of the Peoples would be fully achieved when all societies have been able to establish either a liberal or a decent regime. This underlines the normative presumption that all persons, all human beings, should have the right to live in a society in which their voice is taken seriously, at a minimum by representatives in a consultation hierarchy. Despite these convergences of the Rawlsian consultation hierarchy and the proposal of a human right to voice, his overall conceptualization of human rights on the one hand, but also his explicit emphasis in the 'three observations' that follow the introduction of the idea of a decent consultation hierarchy give reason to ask whether the derivation of a human right to voice understood as an individual right overstretches his intention. Let me show why I think that this is not the case. In his first observation, Rawls emphasizes that in decent consultation hierarchies, groups, not (as in the liberal scheme) individuals, are represented. He explains his preference for the group theoretical standpoint towards the individual's standpoint by arguing that 'the individualistic idea that each person, as an atomistic unit, has the basic right to participate equally in a political deliberation' is not shared by decent hierarchical societies. Because they never integrated the liberal democratic concept of one person, one vote, the dominating view in well-ordered decent societies is that persons belong first to groups such as estates, corporations, and associations:

---

36 Rawls, *The Law of Peoples*, 71.
37 Rawls, *The Law of Peoples*, 4.

> Since these groups represent the rational interests of their members, some persons will take part in publicly representing these interests in the consultation process, but they do so as members of associations, corporations, and estates, and not as individuals.[38]

However, in applying the consultation hierarchy using the fictive example of Kazanistan, he insists on six guidelines, of which the first says that authorities have to consult all groups, and the second that *each* member of a people must belong to a represented group.[39] At this point, Cohen's normative idea of membership meets its Rawlsian base.

In addition and in the context of claiming religious toleration as a criterion for decent societies, Rawls claims that if the adequate representation of the individual's equal (religious) freedom rights cannot be guaranteed "it is essential that a hierarchical society allows and provides assistance for the right of emigration."[40] This justification of the member's right to the "emergency solution" of emigration underlines the emphasis Rawls puts on the protection of the individual person also in his international theory. This concern for the balance of injustice at the individual level is also expressed in his "third observation." Concerning the representation of these members in a consultation hierarchy, who may have long been subjected to oppression and abuse, such as women, he demands that a majority of the members of the bodies representing the (previously) oppressed group must be chosen from among those whose rights have been violated.[41] The main objective of a human right to voice is that every individual is heard in his interests especially in life situations that endanger or constrain material and psychic security and basic needs, and in which the national state does not or cannot provide adequate representation and response to these interests. The very same objective underlines the Rawlsian claim to explicitly account

---

38 Rawls, *The Law of Peoples*, 73.
39 Rawls, *The Law of Peoples*, 77:
   This hierarchy satisfies quite closely the following six guidelines. First, all groups must be consulted. Second, each member of a people must belong to a group. Third, each group must be represented by a body that contains at least some of the group's own members who know and share the fundamental interests of the group. These first three conditions ensure that the fundamental interests of all groups are consulted and taken into account. Fourth, the body that makes the final decision—the rulers of Kazanistan—must weigh the views and claims of each of the bodies consulted, and, if called upon, judges and other officials must explain and justify the rulers' decision. In the spirit of the procedure, consultation with each body may influence the outcome. Fifth, the decision should be made according to a conception of the special priorities of Kazanistan. Among these special priorities is to establish a decent and rational Muslim people respecting the religious minorities within it.
40 Rawls, *The Law of Peoples*, 74.
41 Rawls, *The Law of Peoples*, 75.

for the interests and needs of those who were repressed or are still in danger not to be represented adequately in their political or religious community; as mentioned above, he underlines the urgency of this objective by noting that the right to emigrate serves as an emergency solution for the individual.

4.2.4 Potentials and challenges of a human right to voice

Distinguishing between different moral and political rationales in human rights theory, this book elaborated the importance of the still (implicitly or explicitly for all human rights conceptions) fundamental claim stating that human rights are rights humans have in virtue of being humans. In other words, human rights are rights that gain their normative, public action-inspiring force mainly from representing basic individual or subjective rights claims in their core. A philosophical justification of the moral human right to voice has been elaborated referring to the recognition theoretical rationales from Honneth and Ricoeur. The human right to voice was extracted out of the comparison of the several philosophical contributions to the human right to democracy debate, and it represents a common denominator, namely the shared intrinsic core value of any democratic human rights claim. The predominant rejection of a comprehensive human right to democracy cannot be seen as sufficient reason to deny the ethical human rights value of democracy in general. To avoid throwing the baby out with the bath water, the categorical repudiation of a human right to democracy should be replaced by the promotion of the softer and universally justified moral claim for a human right to voice. This minimal normative core claim can but must not in every country lead to democratic government. Nevertheless, it works as a symbol for every human being under every political regime representing the fundamental right to represent one's basic individual interests and to be heard if one is suffering from severe experiences of injustice at the hands of one's own political and social community. Even in the human rights conception of Rawls, which serves as the representative template for most political human rights conceptions, the consultation hierarchy was successfully shown to explain the priority of a right to voice of each member of a society in terms of a right to freedom of thought and religion. More extensive than Cohen's membership conception, Rawls concedes the right to emigrate as an emergency solution for any individual who finds no adequate representation and protection in his society. The main argument of Rawls against understanding human rights as (liberal) individual rights is argued for from the standpoint of cultural and conceptual differences, saying that decent hierarchical societies never had the individualistic liberal concept of one person, one vote. But the thesis that in some decent countries the people's self-understanding is not based on an individualistic idea or on individual rights claims, but rather on a personal identifications as part of the own society and with the community's shared conception of the good, is challenged by the factual considerable use of the exit option in decent but also other non- liberal states such as outlaw states. If the exit option, in particular the right to emigrate, is as Hirschman points out, a private option taken by individuals who see no other way to realize their fundamental interests in a society or to use the public voice option without putting themselves or their families in danger, this act comes down to nothing less than an individualistic choice. An act of emigration, rightly put in the metaphor of voting with one's feet, which is fully or partly caused by the denial of the voice option, can be interpreted as an act of individualization in the liberal democratic sense of a reconquest of freedom. Touching a broad network of correlations, the human right to voice finally refers to the understanding of the right to emigrate or exit as a normatively justified reaction of the individual. By implication, a meaningful right of exit must also entail an obligation on the part of decent societies to allow entrance. However, this obligation seems not entirely acknowledged in the international community. Altogether, the insights about the human right to voice lead to further questions: Which kinds of violations of a human right to voice should lead to the right to emigrate according to the international law? How should the right to voice exercise influence over the definition of the refugee status in international law? However, that is a story to be continued on another occasion.

References

Altman, Andrew, and Christopher Heath Wellman. *A Liberal Theory of International Justice*. Oxford University Press, 2009.
Arneson, Richard J. "Debate: Defending the Purely Instrumental Account of Democratic Legitimacy." *The Journal of Political Philosophy* 11, no. 1 (2003): 122–32.
Arneson, Richard J. "Democratic Rights at the National and Workplace Levels." In *The Idea of Democracy*, edited by David Copp, Jean Hampton, and John E. Roemer, 118–48. Cambridge: Cambridge University Press, 1995.
Beitz, Charles R. "Human Rights as a Common Concern." *The American Political Science Review* 9, no. 2 (2001): 269–82.
Beitz, Charles R. *The Idea of Human Rights*. New York: Oxford University Press, 2009.
Beitz, Charles R. "What Human Rights Mean." *Daedalus*, On international justice, 132, no. 1 (2003): 36–46.
Benhabib, Seyla. "Gibt es ein Menschenrecht auf Demokratie? Jenseits von Interventionspolitik und Gleichgültigkeit." In *Globale Gerechtigkeit. Schlüsseltexte zur Debatte zwischen Partikularismus und Kosmopolitismus*, edited by Christoph Broszies and Henning Hahn, 404–38. Berlin: Suhrkamp, 2010.
Benhabib, Seyla. "Is There a Human Right to Democracy? Beyond Interventionism and Indifference." In *Philosophical Dimensions of Human Rights. Some Contemporary Views*, edited by Christoph Broszies and Henning Hahn, 191–214. Dordrecht, Heidelberg, London, New York: Springer, 2012.
Bernstein, Alyssa R. "A Human Right to Democracy? Legitimacy and Intervention." In *Rawl's Law of Peoples: A Realistic Utopia?*, edited by Rex Martin and David Reidy, 278–98. Oxford: Blackwell, 2007.
Besson, Samantha. "The Human Right to Democracy – A Moral Defence with a Legal Nuance," CDL:-UD(2010)003:1–25. Frankfurt a. M., 2009. http://www.venice.coe.int/web forms/documents/?pdf=CDL-UD%282010%29003-e.
Buchanan, Allen. *Justice, Legitimacy, and Self-Determination: Moral Foundations for International Law*. Oxford; New York: Oxford University Press, 2004.
Caranti, Luigi. "Human Rights and Democracy." In *Handbook of Human Rights*, edited by Thomas Cushman, 85–99. London; New York: Routledge International, 2012.
Charlesworth, Hilary. "Is There a Human Right to Democracy?" In *Human Rights: The Hard Questions*, edited by Cindy Holder and David Reidy, 271–84. Cambridge: Cambridge University Press, 2013.
Christiano, Thomas. "An Egalitarian Argument for a Human Right to Democracy." In *Human Rights: The Hard Questions*, edited by Cindy Holder and David Reidy, 301–25. Cambridge: Cambridge University Press, 2013.
Christiano, Thomas. "An Instrumental Argument for a Human Right to Democracy." *Philosophy & Public Affairs* 39, no. 2 (2011): 142–76.
Christiano, Thomas. "An Instrumental Argument for a Human Right to Democracy." *Philosophy & Public Affairs* 39, no. 2 (March 1, 2011): 142–76. doi:10.1111/j.1088–4963.2011.01204.x.
Cohen, Joshua. "Is There a Human Right to Democracy?" In *The Egalitarian Conscience: Essays in Honour of G.A. Cohen.*, edited by Christine Sypnowich, 226–50. Oxford: Oxford University Press, 2006.

Cohen, Joshua, and Charles F. Sabel. "Global Democracy?" *International Law and Politics* 37 (2005): 763–97.

Dahl, Robert. "Can International Organizations Be Democratic?" In *Democracy's Edges*, edited by Ian Shapiro and Casiano Hacker-Cordon, 19–36. Cambridge, UK; New York: Cambridge University Press, 1999.

Dahl, Robert. *On Democracy*. New Haven: Yale University Press, 2000.

Dahl, Robert A. *Democracy and Its Critics*. New Haven: Yale University Press, 1989.

"Demokratiegeschichte Schweiz." http://demokratie.geschichte-schweiz.ch/definition-demokratie.html.

Erman, Eva. "The 'Right to Have Rights'." In *Human Rights at the Crossroads*, edited by Mark Goodale, 72–83. Oxford: Oxford University Press, 2013.

Ezetah, Reginald. "Right to Democracy: A Qualitative Inquiry, The." *Brooklyn Journal of International Law* 22 (1997 1996): 495.

Feinberg, Joel. *Rights, Justice, and the Bounds of Liberty: Essays in Social Philosophy*. Princeton, N.J: Princeton University Press, 1980.

Forst, Rainer. "The Basic Right to Justification: Toward a Constructivist Conception of Human Rights." *Constellations* 6, no. 1 (1999): 35–60.

Forst, Rainer. "The Justification of Human Rights and the Basic Right to Justification: A Reflexive Approach." *Ethics* 120, no. 4 (July 2010): 711–40.

Forst, Rainer. "Towards a Critical Theory of Transnational Justice." *Metaphilosophy* 32, no. 1–2 (2001): 160–79. doi:10.1111/1467-9973.00180.

Fox, Gregory, and Brad Roth. "Democracy and International Law." *Review of International Studies* 27 (2001): 327–52.

Franck, Thomas M. "The Emerging Right to Democratic Governance." *The American Journal of International Law* 86, no. 1 (1992): 41–91.

Goodin, Robert E. "Enfranchising All Affected Interests, and Its Alternatives." *Philosophy & Public Affairs* 35, no. 1 (2007): 40–68.

Gould, Carol C. *Globalizing Democracy and Human Rights*. Cambridge: Cambridge University Press, 2004.

Gould, Carol C. *Rethinking Democracy. Freedom and Social Cooperation in Politics, Economy, and Society*. Cambridge: Cambridge University Press, 1990.

Gould, Carol C. "The Human Right to Democracy and Its Global Impact." In *Human Rights: The Hard Questions*, edited by Cindy Holder and David Reidy, 285–300. Cambridge: Cambridge University Press, 2013.

Griffin, Christopher P. "Democracy as a Non-Instrumentally Just Procedure." *The Journal of Political Philosophy* 11, no. 1 (2003): 111–21.

Griffin, James. *On Human Rights*. Oxford University Press, 2008.

Habermas, Jürgen. *Between Facts and Norms*. Translated by William Rehg. Cambridge, Massachusetts: MIT Press, 1996.

Habermas, Jürgen. *Faktizität und Geltung. Beiträge zur Diskurstheorie des Rechts und des demokratischen Rechtsstaats*. Frankfurt a. M.: Suhrkamp, 1992.

Hirschman, Albert O. *Exit, Voice, and Loyalty: Responses to Decline in Firms, Organizations, and States*. Cambridge Mass: Harvard Univ. Press, 1970.

Hirschman, Albert O. "Exit, Voice, and the Fate of the German Democratic Republic: An Essay in Conceptual History." *World Politics* 45, no. 02 (January 1993): 173–202. doi:10.2307/2950657.

Honneth, Axel. *Freedom's Right: The Social Foundations of Democratic Life*. Cambridge: Polity, 2014.

Honneth, Axel. *The Struggle for Recognition: The Moral Grammar of Social Conflicts*. Translated by Joel Anderson. Cambridge: Polity Press, 1996.

Humanrights.ch. "Informationsplattform Humanrights.ch." Accessed October 21, 2014. http://www.humanrights.ch/de/menschenrechte-einfuehrung/was-sind-menschenrechte/.

Kirste, Stephan. "The Human Right to Democracy as a Capstone of Law." *Legal Journal "Law of Ukraine"* 4 (2013): 144–62.

Kohler, Georg. "Otfried Höffe, Demokratie im Zeitalter der Globalisierung." In *Geschichte des Politischen Denkens*, edited by Manfred Brocker, 790–806. Frankfurt a. M.: Suhrkamp, 2006.

League of Arab States. *Arab Charter on Human Rights*. 15 September 1994.

Lister, Matthew J. "There Is No Human Right to Democracy: But May We Promote It Anyway?" *Stanford Journal of International Law* 48, no. 2 (February 1, 2012): 257–76.

Lohmann, Georg. "Demokratie und Menschenrecht." Accessed August 28, 2012. http://www.georglohmann.de/demokratie-menschenrechte.html.

Lohmann, Georg. "Liberal and Republican Understanding of the Relationship Between Democracy and Human Rights." In *DARE in ACTION, Vision and Practice for Democracy and Human Rights Education in Europe*, edited by Margot Brown, Anne-Marie Eekhout, and Yoanna Baleva. Berlin: The Dare Network, 2006.

Lohmann, Georg, and Gosepath, Stefan, eds. *Philosophie der Menschenrechte*. Frankfurt a. M.: Suhrkamp, 1998.

Menke, Christoph, and Arnd Pollmann. *Philosophie der Menschenrechte*. Hamburg: Junius, 2007.

Miller, David. *National Responsibility and Global Justice*. Oxford University Press, 2007.

Miller, David. In *CSSJ Working Paper Series, SJ032*, 1–22. Oxford: Department of Politics and International Relations, University of Oxford, 2015.

Nussbaum, Martha C. "Aristotelian Social Democracy." In *Aristotle and Modern Politics. The Persistence of Political Philosophy*, edited by Aristide Tessitore, 47–104. Notre Dame, Indiana: University of Notre Dame Press, 2002.

Nussbaum, Martha C. "Capabilities and Human Rights," *Fordham Law Review*, 66, no. 2 (1997): 273–300.

Nussbaum, Martha C. "Capabilities and Human Rights." *The Harvard Human Rights Journal* 20 (2007): 21–24.

Nussbaum, Martha C. *Woman and Human Development. The Capabilities Approach*. Cambridge: Cambridge University Press, 2000.

Peter, Fabienne. *Das Menschenrecht auf Politische Partizipation*. Hinterfragt – Der Ethik-Podcast. Philosophisches Seminar der Universität Zürich, 2013. http://www.ethik.uzh.ch/hinterfragt.html.

Rawls, John. *A Theory of Justice*. Original ed., reprint. Cambridge, MA: Belknap Press of Harvard University Press, 1999.

Rawls, John. *Eine Theorie der Gerechtigkeit*. Frankfurt am Main: Suhrkamp, 1979.

Rawls, John. *Political Liberalism*. New York: Columbia University Press, 1996.

Rawls, John. *The Law of Peoples*. 4th ed. Cambridge, Massachussets, London: Harvard University Press, 2002.

Reidy, David. "Philosophy and Human Rights: Contemporary Perspectives." In *Philosophical Dimensions of Human Rights. Some Contemporary Views*, edited by Claudio Corradetti, 23–44. Springer, 2012.

Reidy, David A. "On the Human Right to Democracy: Searching for Sense Without Stilts." SSRN Scholarly Paper. Rochester, NY: Social Science Research Network, April 17, 2012. http://papers.ssrn.com/abstract=2041327.

Ricoeur, Paul. *The Course of Recognition*. Cambridge: Harvard University Press, 2005.

Schnebel, Karin B. "Individuelles und kollektiv ausgeübtes Menschenrecht als Selbstbestimmungsrecht." *Archiv für Rechts- und Sozialphilosophie*, January 2008, 26–46.

Schwarzenbach, Sibyl A. "Rawls, Hegel, and Communitarianism." *Political Theory* 19, no. 4 (1991): 539–71.

Sen, Amartya. "Democracy as a Universal Value." *Journal of Democracy* 10, no. 3 (1999): 3–17.

Sen, Amartya. "Elements of a Theory of Human Rights." *Philosophy & Public Affairs* 32, no. 4 (2004): 315–56.

Sen, Amartya. "Human Rights and Capabilities." *Journal of Human Development* 6, no. 2 (2005): 151–66.

Sen, Amartya. *Rationality and Freedom*. Cambridge, Mass.: Harvard University Press, 2002.

Shue, Henry. *Basic Rights. Subsistence, Affluence, and U.S. Foreign Policy*. Princeton: Princeton University Press, 1980.

Talbott, William J. *Which Rights Should Be Universal?* Oxford: Oxford University Press, 2005.

UN General Assembly. *Universal Declaration of Human Rights*. 10 December 1948, 217 A (III).

Warren, Mark E. "Voting with Your Feet: Exit-Based Empowerment in Democratic Theory." *American Political Science Review* 105 (2011): 683–701. doi:10.1017/S0003055411000323.

Weller, Marc. *Escaping the Self-Determination Trap*. Leiden, Boston: Nijhoff, 2008.

Wenar, Leif. "John Rawls." In *The Stanford Encyclopedia of Philosophy*, edited by Edward N. Zalta, 2013. http://plato.stanford.edu/archives/win2013/entries/rawls/.

Index

autonomy   12–14, 21 f., 36, 45 f., 48, 57, 61 f., 74–76, 89, 92–96, 101, 106, 110

citizenship   4, 9, 11, 16, 68, 83–85, 95
collective right   1, 3, 43

democratic life   30, 103–105
democratic peace   1, 37
democratic theory   4, 77, 110

emigration   109, 111, 114, 116
exit   20, 39, 93, 108–111, 116

freedom   3, 11, 13, 18, 22, 24, 36, 38, 40, 44, 49, 52 f., 58, 60–62, 64–66, 69, 72, 75, 92–94, 101, 104–107, 111, 114 f.

global governance   1, 63, 66 f.
government   1, 3, 6, 9, 11, 19, 21, 23, 27–29, 37, 41, 47, 58, 73 f., 76 f., 87, 90, 94–96, 101, 112, 115

human right to democracy
– HRD   1–4, 6, 9 f., 14, 16, 23, 26, 29–32, 40, 45, 48, 57, 61 f., 71 f., 78 f., 83–87, 93–95, 97, 99–101, 115

individual right   2, 9, 21, 23, 29, 42 f., 61, 93, 95, 101, 113
instrumental moral conceptions   6 f., 14, 94, 97
instrumental political conceptions   6, 14 f., 97
international community   3, 9–11, 14, 21, 26, 29, 31, 35, 41, 57, 69–72, 79 f., 98, 106 f., 116
international relations   14 f., 31 f., 34, 51, 59, 98
intrinsic moral conceptions   6, 14, 35, 43 f., 92, 97
intrinsic political conceptions   6

justice   1, 11–14, 16 f., 19, 23 f., 26 f., 29 f., 39 f., 46 f., 57–59, 64, 66, 72, 81, 84 f., 97, 112

legitimacy   14 f., 26 f., 36, 38, 41, 55, 58 f., 82, 86, 98
liberal
– Liberalism   2, 4, 10–13, 18, 22–24, 27–30, 43, 45, 49–51, 63, 76, 81, 83, 85 f., 91, 95, 106, 113, 115 f.

membership   2, 4, 15–22, 24 f., 29 f., 39 f., 58, 85, 87, 93, 98, 100, 109, 114 f.
minority rights   22
moral   1, 3 f., 6, 8, 10–12, 14–16, 18–21, 23 f., 26, 28, 30 f., 33–38, 40, 43–45, 48, 51–53, 55 f., 58–61, 63, 68–71, 74–76, 78–88, 90–97, 99–106, 113, 115

participation   2 f., 6 f., 9, 11, 16, 18, 20, 27–31, 35 f., 38–40, 43, 46, 48, 50, 53, 60 f., 63, 65–67, 71, 77–80, 83–87, 92, 94–97, 99, 101–105, 109
peace   14, 31, 40, 43, 68–70, 97
politics
– political   1 f., 14, 24, 38, 41, 49, 51, 67, 77, 84

recognition   30, 36, 38, 44, 50, 54–60, 63, 65, 79, 86, 93, 102–105, 115

self-determination   1, 3, 14–16, 18–23, 25, 33 f., 39–41, 55, 58, 61, 63, 68, 71–73, 75, 80, 93, 97, 101, 106, 110
solidarity   103, 105

voice   2, 6 f., 15, 20 f., 23, 39 f., 42, 87, 89, 93–96, 100–102, 104–115

https://doi.org/10.1515/9783110628562-008

www.ingramcontent.com/pod-product-compliance
Lightning Source LLC
Chambersburg PA
CBHW022106160426
43198CB00008B/376